Also by Joseph Kessel

THE LION (1959)

THE ROAD BACK

THE ROAD BACK

A REPORT ON ALCOHOLICS ANONYMOUS

BY

Joseph Kessel

TRANSLATED FROM THE FRENCH BY

FRANCES PARTRIDGE

GREENWOOD PRESS, PUBLISHERS

WESTPORT, CONNECTICUT

Library of Congress Cataloging in Publication Data

Kessel, Joseph, 1898–
  The road back.

  Translation of Avec les Alcooliques anonymes.
  Reprint of the 1st American ed. published in 1962 by
Knopf, New York.
    1. Alcoholics Anonymous. I. Title.
  [HV5278.K4713 1979]   362.2'92   78-9948
  ISBN 0-313-21097-7

First and second printings before publication

Originally published in French as *Avec Les Alcooliques
Anonymes,* © 1960, Librairie Gallimard. Published in
England as *The Enemy in the Mouth* by Rupert Hart-
Davis Limited.

Reprinted with the permission of Alfred A. Knopf, Inc.

Reprinted in 1979 by Greenwood Press, Inc.
51 Riverside Avenue, Westport, CT 06880

Printed in the United States of America

10 9 8 7 6 5 4 3 2 1

CONTENTS

❀

PART ONE

I

Stranger Than Fiction

"My name is John N. and I am an alcoholic."

"My name is Mary S. and I am an alcoholic."

This ritual declaration can be heard echoing through meeting halls all over New York any day of the year and before audiences of every description.

Anyone can come in and listen.

I have heard it myself, repeated week after week, evening, afternoon, and morning.

I have heard it on Park Avenue in a gathering of millionaries; in the Bowery, among the wretchedest tramps in the world; with bohemians and homosexuals in Greenwich Village; in Harlem, among the Negroes; at a congress of doctors, psychiatrists, priests, and eminent judges; on the Manhattan waterfront, surrounded by tough sailors with faces tanned by sun and wind.

"My name is William R. and I am an alcoholic."

◇◇◇

"My name is Agnes B. and I am an alcoholic."

The names were different each time, but the words that went with them were always the same.

I have even heard them in mental hospitals and behind the prison bars of Sing Sing:

"My name is Frank T. and I am an alcoholic."

"My name is Elizabeth F. and I am an alcoholic."

It could be taken as a statement of fact, a painful confession, or a cry of despair, according to the character of the man or woman who uttered it. The speakers might be smartly or poorly dressed, according to their social position. Their manners and voice revealed their education or lack of it. But the origins, culture, clothes, and prosperity of speakers and listeners were not of the slightest importance. They all had one thing in common; a stronger link bound them than social environment, nationality, family, or even love. White or black, rich or poor, illiterate or erudite, they were united by a bond of fellowship, they were brothers till death, just because they had all suffered from the same devouring disease and given themselves over body and soul to the monster's clutches. They had all been down into the depths of the abyss, and if they had managed to return to the light of day among their fellow men, they owed it entirely to this solidarity, this fraternal feeling.

"My name is James W. and I am an alcoholic."

"My name is Louise D. and I am an alcoholic."

The strange litany still haunts me as I write these words. For it was the recurrent refrain running through perhaps the most astonishing and moving journey of exploration that I have ever undertaken in the course of a life devoted to searching after the unusual.

It all began with a chance conversation on the Champs-Elysées, where I ran into Irmgard von Cube, a talented screenwriter who had been working in America for a long while. We had last met in Hollywood in 1948. More than ten years had elapsed since then, but I still remembered the evening we had both spent at the house of a German actor who specialized in terrifying roles.

He owned a small ranch nestling in a narrow valley. A huge St. Bernard lay dreaming beside the glowing fireplace in the almost dark room. The somewhat fantastic and alarming atmosphere of the house made one think of the characters its master usually represented on the screen, although in fact we couldn't have had a gayer, more genial host.

One of the most noticeable of the guests was a huge young man with fair hair and a short curly beard, clear eyes, and an eager expression: Burl Ives. His talents had not yet been exploited by either the movies or the theater. But he was a marvelous singer of the love songs, ballads, and laments he had collected during his life as a wandering musician. He had scoured the United States from Mexico to Canada, from one ocean to the other, traveling in freight trains and jumping down before he reached a station. He had lived in hobos' camps, had warmed himself at their fires, and had known what it was to be hungry and cold and lead a carefree life in the open air.

◇◇

Toward the end of dinner he took up his guitar and sang to us tirelessly, on and on. Old popular songs unfolded their magic for us one by one—songs of the plains, marshes, mountains, and rivers; songs of revelry, of slaves, prisons, and the gallows.

And there were bottles of applejack—that insidious illicitly distilled form of alcohol. I don't remember the coming of dawn very clearly, nor how we all got home.

When I ran into my old friend in Paris, we inevitably started talking about that magical evening and the people who were there.

"All the actors, musicians, and writers who were there that night have gone on with their careers uneventfully enough. On the other hand, our host's wife has had a very strange time of it."

At Irmgard's words, a young, smooth, dazzling lovely face, full of the joy of living, seemed to float before my eyes out of the mists of the past.

"She was drinking a lot," my friend went on.

"She wasn't the only one that night," I said.

"I'm talking about her ordinary, daily behavior. When we saw her she still had the habit under control. But afterwards it got the better of her. First it rocked her, and then it completely capsized her. She didn't know what she was doing any more. She couldn't concentrate on anything: her house, her clothes, herself. The marriage broke up. And then came total collapse. She grew dirty, she grew ugly, she grew old."

"Old?" I said. "At twenty-five?"

"Twenty-four," said my friend. "It happens very quickly. If you never brush your hair, never wash, never eat . . . and simply sink down to sleep under the nearest doorway."

"Was she as destitute as all that?" I asked.

"No, her husband gave her a reasonable allowance. But all the money went on drink and wild escapades. She really was almost mad. They found her more than once driving her car stark naked. We all tried to help her. Her simplicity and childlike charm had won her lots of friends. But we got nowhere. She listened to our advice, accepted our help, and began all over again. She went to the hospital, she went to prison. . . ."

Here my friend's professional instinct caused her to pause dramatically.

"Is she dead?" I asked.

"By no means. She's been saved. She's beautiful, and happier than ever before with a marvelous young man she married five years ago."

"It's impossible!"

"It's quite simple," my friend said. "After a particularly horrifying bout she had a moment of lucidity. It was then she called on the help of Alcoholics Anonymous."

"And did that do the trick?"

"Not in a day, nor even a week, of course. But in the end she was saved. And it was among Alcoholics Anonymous that she met her husband."

I repeated the words mechanically:

"Alcoholics Anonymous . . . Alcoholics Anonymous."

It was not the first time I had come across them. I had once heard some American friends discussing a group formed among people who had been utterly destroyed by drink, and describing how they recovered their physical and moral equilibrium by helping each other to become sober and stay sober.

I hadn't paid much attention. Whose fault it was I don't know, but I got the impression that they were talking about some society of teetotalers with a mania for confessing their sins—one of the many eccentric little sects that are to be found in the United States. It didn't seem to me very surprising that a body of that sort should have succeeded in influencing a mentally unhinged and extremely overwrought young woman. I said as much to my friend. She smiled and replied:

"Very well. Women are always suspect. But here's another case—a man this time, and a talented one."

She mentioned the name of a very well-known and gifted American screenwriter. He had worked for most of the important Hollywood studios at a high salary.

A writer who works in one of these picture factories has to do his job on the spot and under supervision just like a mechanic. And like a mechanic he must be absolutely punctual. Some studios even insist that their most famous writers clock in when they arrive at their luxurious offices.

But the screenwriter in question had been fired from

first one important film company, then another, and then a third. In the end he was taken on by the last of the four largest studios.

For the first week he arrived on time, went to the meetings where films were discussed, produced ideas, wrote some good scenes, and thought up some excellent gags. It was true that from early in the morning on he often had recourse to the flasks of whisky, vodka, and gin with which he filled his pockets and the drawers of his desk. But so long as he did his work, and well, that didn't much matter.

However, on the following Monday he didn't appear till the afternoon. The other screenwriters had taken a liking to him, for he was amiable, gay, and easy to work with, and they succeeded in concealing his absence from the producers all that morning. But when at last he did turn up, they saw that the position was desperate. He could hardly stand and was unable to finish a single sentence distinctly. He had obviously spent the whole weekend drinking. He was far gone in alcoholism.

This had been the reason for so many successive dismissals in spite of his talent. And it doomed him to get the sack from the last studio that had taken him on.

After that he would inevitably go to pieces completely. There had been plenty of other disastrous cases. And he had a wife and two children.

"I was writing screenplays for the same studio," my friend went on. "And I went through agonies on behalf of that wretched man, like all the rest of my colleagues. What was to be done? There was no way of helping him, either collectively or individually. Then one of us thought of Alcoholics Anonymous. But our drunken screenwriter refused to approach them. Only by arguing, begging, and pestering did we finally get him to look in the telephone directory, pick up the receiver, dial the association's number, and say:

"My name is so-and-so; I work at such and such an address. I need your help."

Once again my friend paused effectively:

"And then?" I asked.

"I'll tell you what happened then," she replied slowly. "After a quarter of an hour—not a minute more—one of the producers of the company we worked for came into the room where we all were, took hold of our alcoholic friend by the arm, and said to him very gently: 'Come along, you and I must have a talk.' "

It was the expression on my friend's face as she said these words which conveyed their full significance more than anything else. In my astonishment I exclaimed: "But did that really mean . . . ?"

"Yes," she replied. "It meant that the head producer was a member of Alcoholics Anonymous, that he himself had once been a wreck, done for, sunk, in the gutter; and that he had scrambled out of the abyss into one of the most important posts in Hollywood, thanks solely to the help of other alcoholics who had recovered their sobriety. It meant that in his turn he had now come to the help of a man who was in the process of being destroyed by the same disease. And what's more, he succeeded."

I was silent for a moment. All at once the association I had been so uninterested in appeared in a new light and with a new significance.

"Don't you think it's a marvelous story?" my old friend asked me.

"I think I shall go and study this association on the spot, in America," I said, to myself rather than her.

But I didn't have to wait until New York before my first encounter with a member of Alcoholics Anonymous.

II

The Key

If a reporter wants to make a thorough investigation of a closed world, he needs a key to open it with. That is to say, an introduction with sufficient authority and prestige in this closed world for him to be accepted there without hostility or reserve and for its inmates to treat him not as an inquisitive stranger, observer, or hostile witness, but as one of them.

Only then can he get an accurate view of both details and essentials. Only then will he be able to get to the bottom of things and reach the hearts of the people concerned. The reporter's key is the person who can unlock doors for him into palaces, brothels, revolutionaries' cells, nomads' tents, opium dens, or monasteries.

But here I was, on the point of flying to New York to begin my study of Alcoholics Anonymous, and I still had no key.

I expected to spend much time and effort (some of it useless) trying to overcome the inscrutable politeness, the courteous but adamant refusals, and the suspicious withdrawals with which the people I asked about their terrible battle against their secret failing would naturally defend themselves against my indiscretion. Would I even succeed in getting behind the statistics, graphs, and pamphlets intended for the outside world, to the human reality, the springs of agony and hope that had fed these diagrams and figures?

Fortunately the novelist Irwin Shaw happened to be on his way through Paris. We had been friends since 1943, when we were both in uniform in London together, and I confided my worries to him.

"You're in luck," he said. "A great friend of mine who is a member of Alcoholics Anonymous is on vacation here for a few days. He can solve your problem, if anyone can. He's a journalist, and a first-rate one, too."

When Irwin told me his name, I couldn't conceal my astonishment. I knew his work very well indeed.

"I can't believe it," I said. "Do you mean to say that such a brilliant writer as Harry X. has had to call on the help of the association?"

"He makes no secret of the fact," Irwin said. "I'll call him up."

He put out a hand towards the telephone.

"Wait a second," I cried. "Don't be in such a hurry."

I felt paralyzed by intense embarrassment. How could I possibly interrogate a writer who was a perfect stranger to me about the vice, or disease, or shameful

◇◇

taint that had driven him into the arms of Alcoholics
Anonymous? It would be worse than a professional indiscretion. It would be almost an insult.

"Just as you like," said Irwin Shaw, "but when Harry's
on vacation he does as he pleases. He might easily pack
up and be off tomorrow."

Then I realized that if I couldn't overcome my embarrassment and scruples at this first test, I had better
give up my project altogether, for the situation was
obviously going to repeat itself indefinitely. It was now
or never.

I nodded to Irwin, and he telephoned his friend, who
said that he would be delighted to see me at six o'clock
that evening at his hotel.

Harry X. was tall, thin, and very well dressed, with
a lively manner and youthful movements. There was a
look of permanent adolescence about his sensitive
features.

"Come on out to the terrace. It's such a lovely day,"
he said.

Journalism was in his blood, an instinct with him.
While he talked, he was all the time unconsciously ob-
serving the passers-by, sniffing at them like a hound on
the scent. Now and again he let fall a quick, accurate,
amusing, and pertinent remark that suddenly brought
back to me the look and special flavor of some town I
knew too well to appreciate properly.

We sat down at one of the tables, while the crowds
streamed past us, their leisurely mood in tune with the
fading light.

◇◇

"Paris is more wonderful every time one comes," Harry X. said enthusiastically.

It was then that I noticed the curiously guarded and watchful expression that seemed, as it were, superimposed on his youthful and carefree countenance—an expression of painful, cornered, haunted astonishment. A waiter came to take our order.

"Tea with lemon," said my companion.

The waiter turned to me. I thought my hesitation had been too brief to be noticed, but Harry X. shook his head, smiling amiably.

"I belong to Alcoholics Anonymous," he said, "and I can't touch liquor, but you have whatever you're used to. Or I shall really be offended."

I ordered whisky. I didn't really want it, but I had no choice after what my companion had said. He didn't want his abstemiousness to mark him out from other men.

Now the moment had arrived which I had been dreading since my conversation with Irwin Shaw.

"Why did you join the association?" I forced myself to ask him in a firm voice.

Harry X. answered, as if it were the most natural question in the world:

"Because I should have been sunk without it. Done for."

There was a brief silence while I searched for the least wounding formula with which to question this clearheaded, discriminating, and self-controlled man about the period of his downfall. But Harry X. saved me from my predicament, by saying:

◇◇

"Still, I was a relatively mild case."

Then, without having had to ask a single question, I listened with mingled feelings of relief and surprise, while he told me the history of his alcoholism with complete frankness and simplicity, and at times a curious vein of humor.

Harry X. had begun drinking at the university, as hundreds and thousands of other young men have done in the past and do every year: in the heat and excitement of students' parties; or when taking out girls, when a few cocktails made it easier to break down the initial shyness.

At this time liquor only produced a pleasantly reassuring effect on the young man such as we have all experienced: increased gaiety, self-confidence, and animation, euphoric delight in being alive. It was the same all through his student life and even later on when he became a journalist and swiftly achieved brilliant success in his profession.

A great deal of whisky, gin, and vodka is consumed by newspapermen in the United States. None of his friends were surprised when he began drinking more and more. It seemed quite natural, even to him. His days were happy, his nights rapturous; he found his work easy, and it always met with success.

However, one morning he awoke earlier than usual, bathed in sweat and shivering all over. He was tormented by an unbearable feeling of anxiety. Of course he had had more than one disagreeable, nauseated awakening after getting drunk the night before, but a

shower, some hot coffee, and a few physical exercises
had always straightened him out. This time the tried
remedies were useless. His hands and legs went on
trembling, and—what was worse—he could not free
himself from the anguish of mind that lay like a weight
on his chest—his panicky fear of some imminent disaster.

Although it was still very early, he hurried to the
nearest bar. First one glass, then another. The trembling
stopped, his terror vanished. Everything seemed normal
once more.

"I ought to have realized then and there that alcohol
had ceased to be a means and become an end in itself;
that I wasn't living *with* alcohol but *for* it," said Harry X.

His voice was level and calm, and in his eyes I saw a
faint gleam of irony directed against himself, as he
asked me:

"Do you think many men can admit to themselves
that the degrading, terrible name 'alcoholic' applies to
them, before some major disaster has occurred?"

Harry X. swallowed some of his tea, and said with
the same ironical expression in his eyes:

"And there was no need for me to worry, was there,
now that I had found the cure?"

He went to the bar every morning. He always carried
a pint or two in his pocket, and there were others in his
flat. But drink upset him more and more. He couldn't
control his movements; there were drunkards' quar-
rels, blackouts. It seemed to him—was it illusion or
reality?—that he noticed disapproval and disgust

◇◇◇

among his companions, the well-to-do people he usually went about with. He no longer frequented first-class restaurants and bars or attended parties at fashionable homes. He was drawn instinctively to places and company where no one was shocked by a hiccup, and incongruous laugh, or an obscene oath, or minded seeing a drunk fall flat.

"So one slithers down the slippery slope," said Harry X., "till a day comes when one suddenly begins to hate the witnesses of one's shame—even the most accommodating and complaisant of them. They are obstacles, you see, they form a barrier between the drinker and his drink, the alcoholic and his alcohol. And his real life consists of hours on end spent sitting in the kitchen, dazed, wretched, and drowning, in front of a slowly emptying bottle. . . ."

The avenue lamps had been lit. Harry X. smiled happily as he watched the Parisian crowds go by.

"What pulled you through?" I asked.

"My job," he answered. "However bad a state I was in, I always managed to get my copy to my paper in time, either on my own or with my friends' help. Even if it was poor stuff, it got there, all right. But one morning I looked at the paper and my article was not in. Then I understood. Do you see what I mean?"

I nodded. We belonged to the same profession and were equally devoted to it.

"A great friend of mine, called Bob, had an important job on my paper," Harry went on. "He had been through much the same experience as mine, perhaps worse, and

◇◇◇

Alcoholics Anonymous had saved him. Once and once only he said to me casually: 'When the moment comes, Harry, I'll be delighted to be your sponsor and introduce you to the association.' When the paper appeared without my article in its usual place, I knew that this moment *had* come. I told Bob."

"And then?" I asked.

"I've not drunk a drop of alcohol since."

"But why not?" I exclaimed. "How did you stop?"

"It would be too long a story," Harry X. said. "You must see for yourself, then you'll understand."

He shrugged his shoulders cheerfully and went on:

"Besides, it was extremely easy for me. After I'd been to three or four meetings of Bob's group, I no longer had the slightest craving. My story isn't a very interesting one, as you see; I never went right down into the depths like so many others. It cost me no effort to abstain. A mild case, as I warned you."

His eyes, with their haunted, cornered expression, again drifted away toward the passers-by.

"Why do you stay with Alcoholics Anonymous if you don't need them any more?" I asked.

"First, because no one is ever quite safe from a relapse."

"And second?"

"So that I can help others as they helped me," Harry X. said quickly.

"Does that often happen to you?" I asked.

"As often as to any of the rest," my companion said. "One goes wherever the calls come from. It's just as likely to be a millionaire's house as a hovel. You'll see."

I was suddenly aware that he was impatient to mingle with the crowd and go off into the Parisian night. But I held him back, to explain:

"I'm going to New York to look for stories above everything, really good stories. You know the sort of thing?"

Of course he knew. We were working in the same profession, and the same phrase is used in it, whether in French or English. To a journalist *une belle histoire,* or a good story, has nothing to do with morals or aesthetics. It may apply equally to a monstrous crime, a brilliant exploit, a frenzied outburst of hatred, or a paroxysm of love. A good story may mean Mata-Hari, the sinking of the *Titanic,* or the discovery of penicillin— in fact any human adventure that provides intense and unexpected action and is charged with drama, mystery, gaiety, or genius.

Harry X. laughed quietly.

"Off you go, and don't worry," he said. "There's hardly a single case among Alcoholics Anonymous that doesn't rate as a good story."

He was silent for a moment. His untroubled face suddenly became serious.

"Yes," he said, "You'll find plenty of 'good stories'—and one *very* good one also."

I only understood much later what he meant by this.

"One last question," I asked him. "Can you put me in touch with anyone who will make my search easier?"

"Of course I can," he said. "Bob, my sponsor."

Here was the "key" I took with me to New York.

III

The Key (Continued)

The clanking of Linotype machines, the rumble of rotary printing presses, the endless slithering of teletype ribbon, the ringing of a hundred telephones, and the tapping of a hundred typewriters combine to make up the infernal yet magnificent din of a great daily paper, a noise which to every journalist sounds like the refrain of a well-known song. It assailed my ears now in the offices of the *Herald Tribune* in New York, close to Broadway.

I had made my way across the vast newsroom crowded with young men in shirt sleeves typing out articles at top speed or yelling into telephone receivers.

At the far end, shut off from the main part of the room by a glass partition, sat the man I was looking for, also in his shirt sleeves, also bending over a typewriter.

◇◇

Beside his name I knew nothing about him, except that
he had an important job on the *Herald Tribune* and was
a member of Alcoholics Anonymous.

I found this combination extremely disturbing. I
had only just arrived in New York. This was the first
step in my investigation. And it seemed to me incon-
ceivable and incongruous that a man should hold down
an essential and highly responsible job on a great newspaper and at the same time belong to an association
composed solely of people who had been ruined by
drink. Or at any rate that he should do so openly.

So, having got inside Robert N.'s glass cubicle, I
pitched my voice low and spoke discreetly, as if my business with him was secret and illicit.

"I've come from Paris—Harry X. told me to come to
you—to ask you. . . ."

"Yes, I know, I know. Harry wrote to me about it," he
cried. "Alcoholics Anonymous, isn't it?"

Robert N.'s tone was in complete contrast to my con-
spiratorial, guilty one; and as he had stopped tapping on
his typewriter, these loudly proclaimed words struck my
ears with the force of a confession or a challenge.

I soon saw that I had no need to feel surprised or
embarrassed. Robert N. was talking about his membership in Alcoholics Anonymous with utmost simplicity
and frankness, as if it were the most ordinary thing in
the world and couldn't possibly affect his personal con-
tacts or prejudice him in his career. He went on in the
same key:

"I'm enormously interested in this idea of an investigation of our society by a great French paper. I'll give you all the help I can."

He glanced at the half-filled sheet in his typewriter and said:

"The paper can wait. It's an article for Sunday's edition. Let's go and have lunch!"

Robert N. slipped into his jacket and knotted his tie quickly and carelessly. He was a man of medium height, between forty and fifty. He had light brown hair cut very short, prominent cheekbones, and large deep-set eyes. His candid, thoughtful, sensitive face clearly reflected all that went on in his mind.

He took me to a restaurant only a few steps from the *Herald Tribune* offices, but quite unlike most others in New York. Its dark paneled walls, shiny with age, and the simplicity and masculine comfort of its furniture made one think of some old-fashioned English inn, one of the wonderful Fleet Street pubs.

Everyone there was a journalist. It was a restaurant whose traditions were strong and still very much alive. One of these was hard drinking, as was plainly shown by the faces and voices around the long bar.

As soon as we had sat down at a wooden table, the bartender—a tall, heavily built man with snowy hair and red nose, cheeks, and lips—came over to shake my companion by the hand.

"Hello, Bob," he said warmly. "Still going strong?"

"Well enough, Mike," said Robert N. "No worse than in the good old days."

"That's fine," the bartender said.

He went back to his post. Robert N. followed him with his eyes for a moment.

"The good old days," he said. "I must have known Mike for at least twenty years. What a lot of glasses he's filled for me! And what a lot of drinks we've had together! And how often I've been the last man in the bar!"

There was neither regret nor emotion in his voice, and an amused half-smile flickered over his face. He seemed to be talking about someone else.

The waiter who came to take our order set a deep cup of very black coffee in front of Robert N. before he had even asked for it.

"You see! This is my chosen tipple now," he said cheerfully. "I overindulge in it. But one must substitute one poison for another."

He saw that he had given me an opening for the questions I was burning to ask, and he laughingly put up a hand as if to ward them off.

"I'll answer everything, never fear; I'll come clean, all right. It won't be difficult for me. We Alcoholics Anonymous are a bit exhibitionist, as you'll see for yourself."

He dropped his hand, and went on more seriously:

"But there's one point I'd like to clear up before we begin. It'll be worth it, I assure you. What has been your own attitude to alcohol all your life?"

I was taken off my guard, and didn't answer for a few moments No one had ever before questioned me on the subject. Since my early youth I had quite naturally drunk every form of fermented liquor that came my

way—often, much, in every latitude, and in all circumstances. I had overdone it more than once. I had even
passed out, or reached the stage of being ridiculous and
disgusting. I had awakened afterwards with terrible
hangovers. All the same, I had many more pleasant than
unpleasant memories connected with drink. And when I
remembered all the intensely happy hours of warm and
generous good-fellowship, whether in my squadron or
among the tziganes of Paris, in a Siberian armored train,
a sail boat on the Red Sea, or a hut in Tierra del Fuego,
all due to alcohol—how could I fail to think of it as my
trusty and cheerful companion through life?

I tried to explain this to Robert N.

"I understand that perfectly," he said in a low voice.
"And what do you feel about alcoholics?"

His eyes were still fixed steadily on mine in direct but
friendly inquiry.

Only then did I notice that in spite of their gaiety and
life, their gentleness and shrewdness, those large pale
deep-set eyes were full of painful astonishment and
resignation, anguish transmuted into tenderness and
wisdom. It was this expression in his eyes which forced
me to answer him truthfully.

"I think of alcoholics as people without the wish or
strength to stop in time," I said. "Poor devils who have
lost their will power."

"And I suppose you despise them; they disgust you,
don't they?" Robert N. asked. "The most you feel for
them is pity mixed with aversion?"

He was still gazing at me with a naked, exposed ex-

pression, an expression that seemed to admit everything and understand everything at the same time, and
it was with an effort that I answered:

"Well—yes—that's about what I feel."

Robert N. laughed.

"Please don't be so embarrassed," he said, "it's the
universal attitude towards us."

"It has nothing to do with you in any case," I said
warmly. "You've managed to stop. And stick to it. And
that in a world where the temptations are appalling."

I waved my hand towards the journalists all around
us. They were swallowing their drinks neat and fast.
Every few minutes one of them came up and talked to
Robert N. with a glass in his hand.

"You've shown and are still showing a strength of will
which I greatly admire," I began again with feeling.

"It's not mine alone," said Robert N. "My own will
power would never have been enough."

His eyes all at once lost their look of uneasiness and
suffering, and became clear and serene. A very youthful
smile crossed his face.

"Yet ever since childhood I was told about the harm
done by drink," he said. "Oh, it was nothing to do with
my family, who were as happy, good, united, and respected as any in our little town. It was because of a
man who worked for my father, who was a coachbuilder
at that time, and made horse-drawn vehicles, wagon-
ettes, landaus, victorias, and so on. Yes, a prehistoric
trade."

He laughed almost boyishly, and the innocence of

those childhood days seemed to be reflected in his large pale eyes, as he went on:

"Among the men employed in this modest business there was a splendid old upholsterer, an artist at his job, quite irreplaceable. But he suffered from cyclic alcoholism: he could stay sober for weeks on end and then suddenly a bout would begin. He used to vanish for several days. When my father had urgent orders to fill, these disappearances were disastrous. He would get me to go and find the old man—because he and I were great friends and I was the only one who knew where he hid himself. It was in the cemetery, in a secluded corner between two crumbling tombstones. The upholsterer used to carry two enormous jugs full of whisky there, make himself comfortable, get drunk, go to sleep, wake up, get drunk, and go to sleep again. This would go on until the last drop of liquor had vanished, until the final intoxicated snore. I used to try and catch him when he was asleep; then I would break the jugs and shake him as hard as I could. He was very fond of me, so he used to come back with me to the coachbuilder's workroom. And I felt very proud of myself, and far superior to the old drunkard—"

Robert N. shook his head and laughed again. But this time with savage sarcasm.

"I was still very conceited," he went on, "when I went to college and began drinking myself. After all, I wasn't a village workman. I was an intellectual. I had myself under control, I knew what I was up to, didn't I? And I could take it all right, too! My student friends, and other journalists later on, were all impressed by my head for whisky. I felt I was on top of the world. My alcohol intake was going up all the time, and so was I. There was no one so intelligent, talented, dashing, and irresistible as I was. If ever any unfortunate incident interfered with my social or professional success, it was someone else's fault, of course. *They didn't understand me.* And when my first wife left me, after giving me a son, of course it was her fault. *She didn't understand me.*"

Robert N. gulped down the last of his strong black coffee, ordered another, and went on:

"I married again. At first everything was marvelous. You see, my new wife was an alcoholic herself, and what could be more exciting than to be in love and get drunk together? Afterwards the marriage came to grief. We were never in step with each other. A matter of dosage, or of different nervous wave lengths. Sometimes it would be her turn, sometimes mine. And of course it was always the other one's fault. We parted. . . . Then I really did take to whisky in a big way. Night and day. With the inevitable results: fits of anxiety, shivering, blackouts. It got to such a point that when I was on a reporting job and woke up in a hotel, the first thing I used to do was to reach for the telephone directory. Not because I wanted to make a call, but to see from the name on the cover what town I happened to be in."

The other journalists had been moving about us all this time, constantly going up to the shining counter to have their glasses filled by the huge, florid barman Mike.

"Was it one of your friends who came to your rescue?" I asked, remembering what Robert N. had done for Harry X.

"No," he said. "It was my wife."

His large tragic eyes shone with peculiar brilliance from their deep sockets.

"She had taken refuge with a friend of hers in a small town near Philadelphia," said Robert N. "There she went on drinking more and more, partly from self-pity, partly from a sense of grievance against me. Alone and in secret. Then one day her friend confided to her that she belonged to the local group of Alcoholics Anonymous— it's a much more difficult admission to make in a small town than in New York. She had made up her mind to join for the following reason: one evening when she was returning home completely drunk, her mind a blank, she ran over and killed her own little boy of six, without realizing what she was doing."

Robert N. ordered another cup of coffee.

"Hester—that's my wife—joined Alcoholics Anonymous then, and she begged me to join also. I took her advice. And now we're living together happily again— *really* happy. It's lasted three years."

"Without a single glass of liquor?"

"Without a drop."

"But listen," I exclaimed, "you must really explain: how does the transformation take place, by what means, what stages?"

Robert N. gave me a friendly pat on the shoulder and said:

"My dear man (he called me by my Christian name and from that moment I called him Bob), you and I are veteran reporters. We both know that in our profession there's only one sound rule—to see for yourself. Right?"

"Right," I said.

"Very well, then, where do you want to start your investigation?"

"Wherever you say."

"If I were you," Bob went on, "before beginning to study alcoholics who have become anonymous, in other words reformed, I would get some idea of the distance they've traveled by going to see some of those from whom they were recruited—ordinary drunks, in fact. And in the deepest pit you can find. In the Bowery."

IV

The Human Trash Can

It was night. The immensely long avenue was deserted except for an occasional car gliding along the road, where the hard lights of the street lamps and traffic signals lay blurred as if in stagnant water.

It seemed as though this anemic, unhealthy glow on the surface of the asphalt was reflected within the tall sinister-looking houses lining the avenue. Their windows were bare, without a vestige of curtains, and the same murky, melancholy gleam shone through their dusty, soot-coated panes.

The pavement echoed strangely under my lonely footsteps. A sudden feeling of uneasiness came over me. There was someone walking behind me, and gaining on me too, with dragging, sliding steps. But I quickly got hold of myself. It wasn't yet midnight, and I would soon reach the corner where a bull-necked policeman was stationed, night stick and revolver well in evidence. I walked on at the same leisurely pace as before. Then the man behind me passed me and stopped, blocking my way.

I at once saw that my momentary panic had been quite unjustified. The poor wretch was appallingly thin and his ragged clothes hung grotesquely around him; he would hardly have done for a scarecrow. A child could have pushed him over. A horrible trembling shook his long body, from his corpselike face to his squalid down-at-the-heel shoes. He was gasping from the effort of catching up to me, and every time he let out a breath it brought with it a reek of sour, putrid alcohol.

He gazed at me with the tearful eyes of a sick animal and silently stretched out his hand. I put a coin in it, and he stumbled rapidly off without a word toward one of the innumerable bar doors with chinks of lurid light under them. I went on my way.

But the sudden apparition of this scarecrow had a remarkable effect. A moment earlier I had been quite alone. Now, all at once, ragged unkempt phantoms arose from the shadows and surrounded me. Where had they been hiding until now? I had no idea, but all came up to me begging for money and as soon as they got it rushed off towards some doorway, which revealed as it opened a fresco of nightmarish faces under pitiless lights.

My small change was soon exhausted, but the beggars accepted the fact without grumbling or insistence, and I found myself once again in a silent empty street. However, this time I was able to guess the presence of bodies stretched out in doorways or huddled in corners as I walked on through the apparently deserted streets.

These people, sleeping or lying open-eyed in the dimness, the fictitious night of the city, couldn't even pay the pitiful sum asked for one of the innumerable flophouse beds of the Bowery.

For each of the tall decaying houses on either side of the avenue was filled from roof to cellar with wretched beds where men lay wrapped in their rags and devoured by vermin, saturated with the cheapest liquor, snoring, hiccuping, and raving in their nightmare-ridden sleep. The gloomy light shining down into the avenue came from the windows of these flophouses—vast and terrible barracks providing a last resort in utter collapse and defeat.

How long did I spend inside one of them? A relatively short time, reckoned by my watch. But some experiences seem to be independent of time; one's thoughts stand still, held prisoner by the spectacle of eternal damnation. So it was with me as I stood looking at those miserable wretches stretched on their pallet beds.

When I came out again, the night air seemed so delicious that I was reluctant to leave it for one of the bars that were scattered along the avenue. Besides, which one should I choose? What difference was there between this sign or the next?

At last I pushed open the door nearest to me.

I immediately recognized the smell that greeted me. It was the same as that of the dormitories I had just left—the fetid, sordid bittersweet exhalation of sweating skin, the foul breath that comes from rotting entrails. And I at once recognized the hundred or more men gathered in this huge bar, although I had never seen them before. How could I do otherwise? They were the brothers or doubles of the hideous sleepers I had just been staring at with fascinated horror.

They were all standing. They had no choice, since there wasn't a table or chair in the whole room.

Those who were tired leaned against the dirty peeling walls. The lucky ones propped their elbows on the long counter behind which active barmen were at work. And the rest, the majority, stood with legs slightly apart and arms dangling, as if their feet were stuck with lime to the filthy floor. Were they waiting their turn for a drink? for the money to pay for it? or simply for the useless time to pass?

Their total lack of any occupation, the terrible freedom of their existence on the fringe of the normal world, was visible in all their expressions, whatever their age, size, health, or the state of the rags they wore. There was a common denominator in all their faces: these people had reached the point of no return in their journey through life. They had outlived the faculty of despair. They were abject, pitiful, horrifying—but they were no longer unhappy.

This insensibility took the form of a sort of stupefied torpor in the case of the more far-gone among them, with their skeleton-thin bodies and moribund faces. But others, who were younger or stronger, were still putting up a fight against utter disintegration, and even showing a certain defiance.

"Well, buddy, enjoying your outing?" suddenly said a genial but sarcastic voice from somewhere *above* me. The speaker was so tall that my forehead only reached to his shoulder. He must have been getting on past forty. His skin was tightly stretched over his massive bones. He seemed somewhat less filthy and ragged than his companions, and his green eyes, streaked with purplish veins, looked out with calm cynicism from under his bushy brows, which were red like his overlong hair.

"Well, buddy, having a look at the down and outs?" said this man, who stood a head taller than the other nightmarish figures. "Trouble is, the down and outs are thirsty. You must stand them a drink."

"I'd be glad to," I said.

My gigantic companion elbowed a space for us at the bar, opposite a stocky, heavy-jowled barman.

"Hello, Chuck," said this fellow to my companion. "You doing all right tonight?"

"And how!" said Chuck, winking in my direction.

"Whisky?" I asked him.

"Not me," said Chuck. "I'm not choosy. You're talking to a *wino*, buddy."

I had heard the word before. It stood for an alcoholic who got drunk on the loathsome brews distilled from the refuse of the worst grapes, and sold in the underworld for a few cents a bottle with pretentious names like sherry, port, and Chianti.

Chuck knocked off half his glass, and then instinctively passed the remainder to the man next to him, without even looking at him. This man took a swig in his turn and gave what was left to the next. I made a sign to the barman to go on pouring drinks. A circle had now gathered around us. Nearest to us stood two toothless old men, a creature with such threadlike limbs that he looked like a spider, and a young tramp, still handsome though his face had disintegrated.

"To the guy who treats the down and outs!" said Chuck.

The hand holding the bottle was no longer steady. His voice had become thick. And his rough red face, with its several days' beard, was visibly going to pieces. He was quickly reaching a state of supersaturation.

All the same, there was still something proud, almost noble, in the man's demeanor which was not entirely due to his great height.

"What did you do before—this?" I asked him.

The cynical expression reappeared in his eyes for a moment.

"We down and outs won't sell ourselves for a drop of booze," said Chuck.

And from that moment I ceased to exist for him.

His companions were less proud. One had been a tailor, another a longshoreman, another a chauffeur, another a student. How did they earn their living, or rather their drink, now? It was difficult to say. But there was always the chance of a truck to unload, some cases or furniture to move, a back yard to sweep, or a building site to keep an eye on. Then there was the help they got from their pals; there was borrowing and begging, there were sightseers.

"And we can sell our blood to the transfusion banks," said the student. "That's a regular source of supply." Suddenly the whole place became intolerable to me—its stench, its harsh light, its faces, everything.

Though the vast avenue was empty and the air fresh and cool, I didn't feel free yet. Every glimmering light coming from the windows of a flophouse suggested the candles at a wake. Every sign pointed the way to a bar like the one I had just fled from. And there was no end to them.

Bars and flophouses, flophouses and bars, rags, vermin, spectral figures for mile after mile—that was the Bowery, a town within a town, a world of outcasts, a human dead end, a trash can for bodies and souls.

"You want to know what the population of the Bowery is?" Bob said to me. "I don't know the exact figures. But there must be thirty thousand or so. And there's a replica of it in Chicago, Los Angeles, San Francisco, New Orleans, in fact in every large or medium-sized town. 'Skid row' is what they call them. You'll find the same sort of human refuse in all of them.

"However, these underworld regions represent only the final and most spectacular stage of alcoholism in America. I could take you to hundreds of discreet, luxurious bars where thousands of rich, important, influential men look in every morning on the way to the office and hastily knock off several glasses of whisky, gin, or vodka, because they *simply cannot* start the day's work without it.

"Then there's the great army of solitary drunks, and those in prisons and lunatic asylums.

"Have you any idea how many men and women in the United States are being destroyed by alcohol? I'm not talking of moderately hard drinkers, but of those who are in really grave danger, either mentally or physically. The most reliable estimate puts the number at between five and six million."

Bob paused to give me time to get used to this figure and absorb its significance. Then he went on:

"Yes, five to six million human beings, all of whom are in danger of ending up in the Bowery one day, or in some skid row or other. Because, believe me, the slope is a very steep one and the barriers go down with horrifying speed and ease. Professional pride, family feeling, dignity, personal cleanliness, and the instinct of self-preservation all give way one after the other, until nothing at all is left but the need to be free to drink— anything, anyhow, anywhere. They all finish in the gutter. You've no idea what a lot of schoolteachers, bankers, doctors, journalists, and lawyers are to be found in the Bowery."

Bob smiled, but there was an expression in his large eyes which was painful and alarming to see.

He went on slowly:

"If it hadn't been for Alcholics Anonymous, I think I should have been there, too."

◇◇◇

I remembered the flophouse and the bar, and couldn't help shuddering.

"Poor wretches. There's no hope at all for them, then," I said.

This time Bob's smile was spontaneous and surprisingly youthful.

"You think not?" he asked.

He took a small yellow-covered booklet out of his pocket and handed it to me, saying:

"Here you have the dates and addresses of the weekly meetings of all the different groups of Alcoholics Anonymous in New York. There are more than three hundred, and anyone can go to them."

He turned the pages and underlined some words with a red pencil.

"You'll find an answer to your question *there*," he said.

The dark outline of the great shed loomed up depressingly, emphasizing its dreary purpose and situation. It was a municipal night shelter. And almost at its very door ran that great road to ruin, hopelessness, and chronic, abject, desperate drunkenness—the Bowery.

It was eight o'clock in the evening. The main hall of the shelter was poorly lit and smelled of dirt, foul breath, and dishwater soup. A few miserable ragged skeletons, with stooping shoulders and bristling or bearded faces, dragged their shapeless shoes over the flagstones. I tried not to look at them. I remembered the hours I had spent among their fellows last night in the flophouses and bars of that damnable avenue. I had

come for one thing only, to attend the meeting of Alcoholics Anonymous which was due to take place that day.

The meeting room was painted a toneless gray. In
the middle were some rows of chairs on which were sitting about twenty men of all ages. They came from the
Bowery; there could be no doubt of that. The sole exception was a Negro, freshly shaven and wearing a new
suit. However, drink had got him, just as it had the rest
of the audience.

Some showed no signs of drunkenness except a dim,
drifting look in their eyes and a vacant grin; others had
reached a state of sodden somnolence or were muttering in frightened or angry tones. But however drunk
they were, they were making an obvious and pathetic
effort to "behave themselves," that is, to be as restrained
and sensible as possible.

A side door opened to admit two men who walked
up to a table in front of the audience. One was young.
He was wearing a worn, skimpy suit that had obviously
come from a secondhand clothes store but been carefully brushed and pressed. His lined, earnest, and remarkably handsome face suggested both ill health and
inspiration.

The other was very different: about fifty, well
dressed, clean, and muscular. The confidence with
which he moved, his lively expression, and the
friendliness of his smile all bore witness to an uncom-
monly well-balanced personality.

"My name is John M. and I am an alcoholic," he began, frankly and almost gaily, breaking the profound

silence. "As chairman of this meeting, I have great
pleasure in introducing this evening's speaker:
Toddio."

John M. patted the younger man on the shoulder and
went on:

"It's not long since he knocked off liquor. You could
tell it from his face, couldn't you? And this is the first
time he's spoken in public. So give him a fair hearing,
boys, and make it easy for him. Your turn now, Teddie!"

The young man clenched his teeth, so that his jaw
jutted out under his gaunt cheeks. His Adam's apple
moved up and down his thin neck, and his eyes seemed
hollower and more brilliant than before.

"My name is Ted C. and I am an alcoholic," he said
in a low voice.

He drew in a long, painful breath and then all at
once plunged headlong into his speech.

I had never before been to a meeting of this sort,
and I expected to hear moralizing and propaganda.
Nothing of the kind. It was simply the story of a life.

Ted C.'s parents had been ordinary people, neither
better nor worse than most. He had done only moderately well at school. After being apprenticed to a car-
penter, he had begun to earn a decent wage. Like everyone else, he liked to change his clothes when the day's
work was done, and go dancing or to the movies. Life
was pleasant and easy for this very normal young man.

So far the audience hadn't shown much interest,
though some followed the story with mild curiosity and
partial attention. Others tipped back their chairs,

yawned, or scratched themselves. The Negro smiled benignly, showing his gleaming teeth. Close to him, an old drunk whose skin hung loosely on his enormous frame kept laughing derisively. Since he hadn't a tooth in his head, his lips curled back to reveal horrifyingly empty, jagged gums. His bloodshot eyes were full of spite against the universe.

Suddenly I became aware of a change of mood in the audience. The sleepers went on sleeping, of course, but the rest were sitting up straighter, with their necks stretched forward, and had stopped fidgeting and yawning. The Negro wasn't smiling any more.

This was because Ted C. had now begun to describe his first encounter with drink. His voice had become strong, confident, and vital; leaning with both fists on the table, he presented the audience with a face transformed with enthusiasm. He seemed possessed. He was concerned only with his failing, the disease that had ravaged all the other men surrounding me—the down and outs of the Bowery.

"One Saturday evening I went to a bar with some pals," said Ted. "Everyone stood a round of drinks. Nothing wrong in that, was there? A guy has a right to a bit of fun when the week's work's over and he has some money in his pocket. . . ."

The only trouble was that whereas drink brought relaxed high spirits and stimulating warmth to his friends, he had passed out and had to be taken home. Was it just that he wasn't used to it, that he was taken off his guard? It was the first time, certainly.

But then, why did he do the same thing the following Saturday? Why had he felt compelled to spend his last cent on making himself insensible? And every Saturday afterwards?

"I was different from the rest. I had no head for alcohol. But how was I to know?" exclaimed Ted. "As soon as I began to drink, I was happy; there was a warm glow in my stomach and in my head. But that wasn't enough for me. I wanted something stronger, warmer. One glass led to another, and the gaps between grew shorter . . . until the moment when I knew nothing more."

A half-stifled whispering close to my shoulder mingled with Ted C.'s words.

"That's it . . . that's exactly the way it is."

It was the man next to me, the young Negro, though he was hardly aware of what he was saying. His thick lips and pink tongue moved of their own accord; so did his moist, innocent eyes.

"At first these bouts only took place on Saturdays," Ted C. went on. "Then I found excuses to get drunk on other days of the week as well. And, you see, I'd become pretty touchy. No one understood me. The whole world was against me: my mother, if she made a remark; my employer or his clients, whenever they found my work anything short of marvelous; a girl, if she preferred to dance with someone else. Then I would have a drink to console myself or out of a sort of revenge. And that drink became a whole bottle and then another, and there I would be, blind drunk."

The young man paused, and mopped his damp forehead.

"It took a long time to live my story, though it's short enough to tell," he went on. "I depended on liquor to give me the courage to go to the workshop, and then to steady my hand. I was sodden with it all day long. I don't know if it was my family who were ashamed of me, or I of them, but anyway I left them. No nice girl would go out with me; I drank too much. In the end my long-suffering employer fired me. I was a good worker and I got other jobs, but never for long because of the drink. I had to have more and more of it and was out of work much of the time, so I bought the cheapest I could get—really poisonous stuff. At that time nothing seemed to matter any more—clothes, my appearance, my health. I had sunk to Bowery level."

Ted C. uttered the name of the terrible avenue quite naturally, without the slightest emphasis. The poor wretches in the audience heard it in the same spirit, except that their despondent faces began to show obvious signs of interest. The boy who was talking was one of them. The burly old man with the expression full of hatred even mumbled some sort of agreement between his toothless gums.

But the Negro muttered: "I've not yet sunk to the Bowery. . . . Not me."

"Shut your trap!" grumbled the old alcoholic, threatening him with a gnarled, misshapen fist.

Ted C. started talking again quickly:

"Perhaps you boys and I may have come across each

other in the Bowery. One can't see who's in every corner
of those bars and lousy rooming houses! You've known
that way of life as long as I have. I did a few odd jobs,
cadged drinks, begged, and sold my blood to the transfusion banks. And I had a bit of luck, too: I worked as a
gravedigger two or three days a week—graves for
paupers, of course, people who end up in the morgue."

"Jesus Christ!" whispered the Negro.

"Everything was all right," Ted C. continued. "I could
drink as much as I liked. But one day, as I was digging
a grave with another fellow, he said to me: 'The un-
dertaker's men told me this guy we're preparing for now
is a down and out from the Bowery. They picked him up
stiff off the pavement—he'd ruptured his liver with
drink.' "

Ted C.'s eyes traveled around his ragged audience,
with their worn, ravaged faces. He said in a low voice:

"I suddenly felt weak—so weak that I had to lean on
my shovel for support. I remembered that I'd given up
eating, that I only weighed ninety pounds. I saw myself
lying in a hole in the ground, with my liver, kidneys, or
heart shot to pieces. And I wasn't yet thirty. I felt more
afraid than I'd ever been in my life before. And more
than ever before I longed for a good strong drink. I
hurried off to get the pay due me for digging that
grave, and off I went to the nearest bar. But at the
door a thought struck me: 'If you have that drink, you
won't stop till you're in a hole in the cemetery, and that'll
be soon.' All the same, I knew I hadn't the strength to
fight the booze by myself. I needed help. Then I remem-

bered what I had been told about Alcoholics Anonymous.
I went to look for them, and I found them."

Ted C. wiped his damp forehead with the back of his
hand. His face was taut and lined from his exertions,
and the bones looked as if they must come through
the skin. But his eyes were steady and full of fierce
energy.

"I won't try to pretend it was pleasant," he said. "But
are fits of horrors, attacks of trembling, ulcers, vermin, and d.t.'s pleasant? I suffered, of course, but it
was once and for all. And Alcoholics Anonymous helped
and supported me all day and all night. They provided
the ways and means to get through the worst of it.
Now I've got a job, and I enjoy my food; I've even
made some friends. I've begun to live again. That's
all. . . ."

Ted C. stopped speaking suddenly. John M.—who
had opened the meeting—put his arm around the
young man's shaking shoulders and said:

"Thank you, Teddie. On behalf of us all."

Then, to the audience: "And thank you, too, boys.
We'll meet again next week."

The bowery tramps got up from their chairs. I noticed traces of some obscure emotion in the faces of two
or three. But the general attitude was indifferent, or
defiant, or even hostile. The corpulent old soak with
the toothless gums spat noisily as he passed Ted C., and
muttered:

"Softly! Dirty hypocrite!"

Then he remarked sarcastically to John M.:

◇◇

"I've only come for the coffee—nothing else! Like I always do."

"O.K., Tim, you'll find the coffeepot in the usual place," was the cheerful reply.

The old alcoholic shambled off into the next room, followed by most of the others. But three, whose pale haggard faces had seemed for an instant lit and warmed from within, stopped and spoke in low voices to John M.

The young Negro sitting beside me hadn't stirred. Suddenly he said to me:

"That boy was really good, wasn't he? It was all true, just like he told us. It's good fun and you're having a little spree, and suddenly there you are in the gutter. All your money gone on drink, and your clothes and shoes as well. I've got a good job at the docks, you know, and I'm fond of nice clothes, and the girls like me. And I've a wife and two kids as well. But I can't seem to help it. I go into a bar for a drink, and I don't leave till they throw me out. Pretty rotten, isn't it? Those guys are dead right," and he pointed to John M. and Ted C.

There was a tremor in the Negro's warm, ingenuous voice. Large tears were glistening in his eyes. He slipped a hand into his pocket and pulled out a handkerchief, but he didn't use it. A slight rustling noise caught his attention, and he stared in astonishment at two green bills lying crumpled in his pink palm.

"Christ!" he whispered. "I've still got two dollars left."

His face was cracked in two by an enormous grin.

◇◇◇

Then he winked one still moist eye, now shining with childish mischief, and exclaimed:

"I'm off to have a quick one, only one. . . ." And he vanished.

No one but John M. was left in the room now. He came up to me and said in a friendly voice:

"I know who you are. Bob N. told me to expect a French journalist at our next meeting. Well, what do you make of it all?"

I answered with another question:

"Do you really hope to save many of these down and outs from the Bowery?"

"Why not?" said John M. "Alcoholics Anonymous saved me."

"You? You?"

I realized I had raised my voice, and went on more quietly:

"You're joking! You and those. . . ."

"Go on! Say it!" said John M., laughing. "Those tramps, those bums, that unspeakable rubbish—anything you like to call them, and then some. I was one of them for a long time, yet now I give orders to others and am my own boss. But I once used to sell my blood as they do to buy wine—port if possible, because I believed it thickened the blood—Bowery port, you understand."

John M. laughed louder still, as though he had remembered a splendid joke.

V

Mink and Sable

Robert N. was waiting for me at the corner of 60th Street and Park Avenue, that is to say, in the very heart of one of the smartest, richest districts of New York. Here were the newest and finest skyscrapers, rearing their façades of concrete, glass, and metal toward the clouds. Vast wealth and huge businesses were housed in these transparent cliffs, and when darkness fell their topmost lights seemed to merge with the stars.

"I'm taking you to a meeting of the Rhinelanders group," Bob told me; "they get together once a week all the year round, like all the five hundred New York groups. These groups are the essential organs, the life cells of the association."

"Then, yesterday's meeting. . . .?" I began.

"No," Bob said, "the tramps in the municipal shelter don't constitute a group. The only members of Alcoholics Anonymous you saw there were John M. and the speaker he brought with him. The audience was made up of drunks still in the toils of their disease and under the spell of liquor. If John M.'s rallying cry encouraged any of them to stop drinking, why, then he would join one of the groups."

"How would he choose?" I asked.

"He'd please himself. He'd follow his sponsor if he had one. Or it might be according to where he lived, or to his social or intellectual background. And he could change when he liked, as I did myself. I left the Park Avenue group and joined Greenwich Village."

"Here we are," said Robert N. when we had gone a little way down 60th Street.

He stopped in front of a church—it was Christ Church.

"Nothing to be afraid of," he said, laughing at my involuntary movement of recoil. "I'm not taking you to hear mass, or a sermon. Nor to a pious conclave. Some groups prefer to meet in churches because they're so large and can be hired for a small fee; others meet in schools, private clubs, or the halls of asylums or re-formatories."

"What! In madhouses and prisons?"

"I've often been to meetings in both," said Bob calmly. "And you will, too, I assure you. But one thing at a time. Tonight you must make do with my old group, the Rhinelanders."

Bob went up to a small door on the left of the main portal of the church. Before following him inside, I couldn't resist saying:

"You know, rightly or wrongly, in France we have

◇◇

a strong prejudice against all antialcoholic sects, temperance societies, and prohibition leagues, whether religious or not. They seem to us unnecessary and ridiculous."

"So they do to us," said Bob cheerfully.

We went down into a basement that had, I must say, no flavor of religion about it. The walls were painted white, and it was brilliantly lit. On the right I saw a very large kitchen, glittering with the most modern equipment; several women were busy making coffee in enormous electric coffeepots, setting out piles of biscuits and cakes, and sorting cups and saucers. The sound of voices was coming from behind a half-open door on the left. Bob pushed it open, saying:

"The real meeting doesn't begin for another hour and in a much larger hall. But I wanted you to see what we call the 'newcomers'' meeting, which always comes first. It's for people who have only been members of Alcoholics Anonymous for a very short while, and for those who haven't yet made up their minds to join."

The word "newcomer" automatically suggests youth. But it didn't apply to the dozen or so people in the room Bob led me into. Their ages, as a matter of fact, represented every stage of life, from the boy only just past adolescence, sitting in a stupor with his chin on his hollow chest, to the old gray-haired lady with bloodshot eyes and an erratically shaking head. There were more women than men.

All of them were sitting in folding metal chairs arranged diagonally across the room, and opposite them

in a red leather armchair was an old timer—a qualified member of the Rhinelanders group.

He was a pleasant-looking, strongly built, confident
man of about forty. The careless ease with which he
wore his well-tailored flannel suit showed that he was
used to luxury.

All this made what he was saying the more astonishing. For as I came into the room this well-dressed,
smooth-faced man who smelled of shaving lotion and
expensive cigars was describing the utter destitution,
degradation, and bodily and mental neglect in which
he had lived for years because of drink.

"At the bottom of the ladder. Right in the depths of
the pit," the old timer was saying as he sat at his ease,
with legs crossed, in the red armchair. "It would be
difficult to sink any lower than I did. If I got out, so can
you. It's only a question of making a start, you know—
of *wanting* to make a start. After that you'll be helped
by people exactly like yourselves, whose problems were
once the same as yours."

He uncrossed his legs, recrossed them with the right
over the left, and went on:

"Above all, don't make tremendous resolutions and
pledges. Don't swear you'll never drink again. The mere
idea puts a man in a panic. Simply say to yourself: 'I
won't touch liquor for the next twenty-four hours.'
That's all. Twenty-four hours. Don't think a moment further ahead. And when you've got through the first day
safely, say to yourself: 'Now another twenty-four hours.
It's not so very terrible, I've done it once already. After

that, we'll see.' First rule: live twenty-four hours at a
time. Second rule: come to our meetings as often as
possible. You've got the booklet and the list of meetings?
Anyone who hasn't need only ask me."

Other simple, trivial pieces of advice followed—con-
siderations of hygiene, regime to be observed, medicines to be avoided. They were delivered in a neutral,
toneless voice. Did this air of detachment come from a
desire not to dramatize and alarm, or was it just force
of habit? It hardly mattered: the speaker's attitude and
tone of voice removed any flavor of pity from his words.

On the other hand, his listeners hung on his words
with anguished, eager, almost tragic attention. They
had scarcely emerged from the abyss; they were still
battling with the terrible craving that had ruined their
lives. They clearly belonged by birth and education to
the same social class as the man who was addressing
them. But their clothes were made of humbler material
and were shiny and threadbare. The women, in particular, seemed to have made a timid, pathetic attempt to
look clean and respectable, as the poor do when they
have to appear in public. But the trouble they had taken
with their faces and their hair hadn't succeeded in
effacing the terrible stigmata of their failing—grayish
complexions, flabby flesh, discordant features, tics,
tremors, and above all their fixed, hunted, and inscrutable expressions.

These "newcomers" taking their first uncertain, difficult steps along the road that might lead them out of
hell, and the others who were still shrinking from em-

◇◇

barking on it—listened to the old timer, the man who
had been saved, with conflicting emotions, which were
nakedly and distressingly displayed on their alcohol-
ravaged faces. There, right in front of their eyes, sitting in a red chair, was a miracle. They longed to believe
in it with all the strength and faith they were capable of;
yet they were tormented by anxiety: would they have
enough will power, patience, strength, and courage to
do likewise?

There were two women sitting near me who showed
this conflict between hope and anguish very clearly.
They were still young and good-looking; yet their
sensitive faces were distorted by drink: shriveled
bluish eyelids, deep eye sockets, hard creases at the
corners of their mouths, cachectic thinness. They were
chain-smoking (nearly every member of the audience
had an ash tray on his knee, or within reach), and their
long, bony, tobacco-stained fingers were never still One
of them wore a freshly ironed dress with several burns
on it. She must have collapsed into a drunken stupor
more than once with a cigarette in her mouth.

I distinctly heard her mutter to her neighbor in a
feverish, gasping voice:

"He knows what he's talking about, all right: he's
been through the same as we have. He's even had it
worse, he's sunk lower. And look at him now."

A few minutes later:

"But what does that prove anyway? I've stopped
drinking several times myself; I kept sober for long
stretches. So did you. And we had money, plenty of it.

We had the best doctors and psychiatrists. All the same, we began again . . . and worse than ever."

She was silent, and her face remained shut and sealed by despair, until renewed hope brought it to a sort of hallucinated life again, and she whispered to her friend:

"But we were alone then, we didn't have these people to help us. Can they really help us as much as all that? And if so, how?"

The old timer uncrossed his legs, took a long thin cigar from his pocket, and carefully lit it. Between two puffs, he said:

"Well, there you are! I think that's all. However, I'm sure to have left out some problems of interest to one or another of you. Ask me any questions you like. I'll answer as best I can."

There was a long, embarrassing silence. I looked at the young woman whose anxious remarks I had just overheard. She had so many questions to ask, things she wanted explained. For a second she seemed on the point of saying something, but no sound came from her trembling lips. I saw other faces burning with the desire to ask questions. However, not a soul among the audience had the courage to take the plunge.

"Good," said the old timer, getting up from his red armchair. "Good. The meeting is over, and also it's nearly time for the open session. Any of you who'd like to stay on will be welcome."

While everyone got to his feet with a great scraping of metal chairs, Bob said to me:

"The newcomers haven't got used to discussion yet, nor to coming out with their problems and troubles in public. They would be embarrassed and ashamed to declare themselves alcoholics. They can't forget the contempt the word arouses in most people."

My companion laughed silently.

"But give them a little time, and there'll be no stopping them. . . ."

The newcomers had left the smoke-filled room. Only the very young man still lay back in his metal chair; he had been sound asleep since the beginning of the meeting. Bob looked at him for a moment with a curious half-smile, made up of pity, tenderness, understanding, and complicity, and said:

"He was afraid to come, afraid of being forced to commit himself. So he took precautions in advance and got tight."

"Why is he here then?" I asked.

"Because he also desperately wants to stop drinking," said Bob. "And, you know, even the state he's in now needn't necessarily be an insuperable obstacle. I've seen a man stagger into two, three, five meetings completely drunk, and flop into a chair at once, speechless and seemingly incapable of hearing a word that's said. Yet there suddenly comes a moment when he has understood, he's been caught, he's become one of us. How? Why? You must look among our unconscious impulses for an answer."

There was no one left in the smoky room except ourselves and the sleeper. Bob went up to him and shook him very gently. The young man opened his eyes with an effort.

"Everyone's gone, buddy," said Bob kindly. "Come and have a cup of black coffee in the kitchen before the group meeting."

"Thanks," said the young man, "that's very kind of you."

His voice was thick and hesitant, but he spoke with an educated accent.

"Hold on a minute," he said. He made several efforts to sit up straight, but his legs refused to support his weight. His reaction to this was to take a flat bottle half-full of whisky from his pocket and swallow its contents greedily; then, still moving like an automaton, he felt in another of his pockets and found a second flat bottle. Having thus recovered his strength and freedom of action, the young man stood up, pulled his shirt down, readjusted his tie, and combed his black hair. His face was pale, refined, and extremely sensitive.

"Are you coming to the group meeting?" Bob asked him.

"I'm going to my usual bar," said the young man defiantly.

"All right, see you another time," Bob said cheerfully.

The young man went out without another word.

"Do you think he'll come back?" I asked my companion.

"Perhaps never, and perhaps for good."

◇◇◇

We followed a series of underground passages toward the sound of a great many voices, which grew louder with every step we took.

"The public meeting will be starting any moment now," said Bob.

It was the first time I had been present at a meeting of this sort, and I fully expected to find it surprising. So indeed I did, but in a way I had not foreseen, and to such an extent that for a moment I felt I must have come to the wrong place.

How was I to believe that this room Bob led me into was part of a church—this huge, white, anonymous, noncommittal rectangle, empty of any objects of worship and furnished with long rows of chairs and a platform bristling with microphones?

And, above all, what could these people have to do with anguish of mind, physical and mental collapse, poverty—in short with the tragedy of alcohol? It was not only that they showed no bodily or nervous signs of the disease, but they seemed to exude health. Far from looking sad, depressed, or anxious, they were overflowing with gaiety and vitality.

And as for their material circumstances—instead of the signs of deterioration I had expected, there was security, wealth, and even exceptional luxury all around me.

One saw it in the men's suits, ties, and bearing; and even more in the quality of the women's dresses, furs, and jewels.

Since the meeting hadn't yet begun, people were exchanging friendly greetings, calling each other by their Christian names, and gathering in talking, joking, laughing groups. A cheerful but calm, restrained, and well-bred buzz of conversation filled the white hall and gave it an atmosphere of pleasant lightheartedness approaching frivolity.

"What have you brought me to?" I couldn't help asking Bob. "A fashionable soirée? A cocktail party?"

"Perhaps—but without any drinks," he said.

He was much amused by my astonishment.

"Don't forget we're in the wealthiest part of Park Avenue," he went on. "This group—the Rhinelanders—which was the first I ever joined—forms part of a well-defined social circle. Most of the members hold important jobs in advertising, radio, television, the theater, and movies, journalism, or public relations. Nearly all of them, men and women alike, are extremely rich and handle even larger sums than they own."

Bob laughed heartily, adding:

"Do you know what our nickname for the Rhinelanders group is? Mink and Sable. . . ."

"But where are the alcoholics, then?" I asked.

My companion surveyed the assembly of between one and two hundred people, all earning or handling many thousands of dollars. His large pale deep-set eyes gave the impression of seeing and understanding the essential nature of people and things better than most of us; but when they again met mine, they were deeply serious.

"I don't believe," he said slowly, "no, I really don't believe that there's a single man or women here tonight whose life has not been ravaged by drink. I know some of them have fallen as low as the Bowery."

"The Bowery . . . the Bowery," I murmured, incredulously. That dead-end avenue, that infernal last resort of down and outs, that abominable refuge of alcoholic despair.

"Do you mean to say that some of the people I see here have lived in the Bowery?"

"Why yes," said Bob.

But at that moment all conversation ceased, and the meeting began.

A man stepped on to the platform and went up to the microphone. He was middle-aged, well groomed, and strongly built. He wore a beautifully cut blue suit, a white silk shirt, a quiet tie, and cuff links set with precious stones.

"The president of the Rhinelanders group, and an important publicity agent," Bob whispered in my ear.

"My name is Warner F. and I am an alcoholic," said the president.

Then:

"I take great pleasure in introducing our leader for this evening."

Bob whispered hurriedly:

"The mechanism of these meetings is always the same. Someone from another group is chosen by the president to direct and stimulate the meeting, and he in turn recruits three speakers from his own or from other groups. This means there is a ceaseless flow of fresh information and interest."

The leader now stood beside the president on the platform. He was thinner and more alert-looking, but dressed just as carefully and expensively.

"He has a huge advertising business," Bob told me.

"My name is Charles R. and I am an alcoholic," said the leader with a dazzling smile. "I do hope my friends who will talk to you tonight won't disappoint you."

The first speaker was a thin, dark young man with restless eyes and nervous gestures.

"My name is Bruce P.," he said, "and I am an alcoholic."

The ritual formula didn't come to him as easily as it had to the last speaker. He had obviously uttered it less often in public and was not used to it yet; it was still impregnated with bitterness and violence for him. It was plain also that he didn't belong to the same social class as most of the Rhinelanders.

In spite of this—or possibly because of it—as soon as Bruce P. began to speak a remarkable change came over the audience. The frivolity and conventional worldliness which had held sway a few moments before vanished entirely.

It was as if their features had become sharper, were wiped clean, and exposed in all their nakedness. A strange look of terror came into their eyes, terror of some hidden but ever-present, serious, imminent danger. Their distress stripped these people of their security, wealth, assurance, and unconcern at one blow, unmasked them as it were, revealing the deeply hidden truth beneath.

But a part, and the best part, of this painful truth was to be seen in their sensitive sympathy and brotherly feeling for this strange young man from another world, who had only one thing in common with his rapt listeners: the disease of alcoholism.

He was telling his life story undramatically, in short dry staccato sentences. He came from a humble family. How and where he had first picked up the taste for drink and then the need for it, he didn't know. It had seemed to come suddenly, of its own accord. In any event, by the time he got a job that really suited him, with an airline, he was already following a well-established routine. Up at six, he breakfasted off two vodkas and two ginger ales before going to the airport. As soon as he got there, he had two more vodkas in the passengers' bar. He couldn't have got through his day in the office without drink. Luckily the company allowed for several short breaks in the day's work, for coffee or to go to the washroom. In every break Bruce hurried to the bar. Of course, the airline personnel were not allowed to drink there, but Bruce got over this difficulty by slipping a tweed jacket (which he kept in the cloakroom) over his uniform. So it went on until five o'clock, when he was at liberty once more.

"After that, I could keep myself going until dinnertime by means of cocktails, of course. And then, at last, I could start drinking seriously."

⟡⟡⟡⟡⟡⟡⟡⟡⟡⟡⟡⟡⟡⟡⟡⟡⟡⟡⟡⟡⟡⟡⟡⟡⟡⟡⟡⟡⟡⟡⟡⟡⟡⟡⟡⟡⟡⟡⟡

The audience laughed sympathetically; they appreciated the joke. And the young man with gray hollow cheeks and distraught eyes laughed, too. Then he went on with his story.

He was fired by a dozen different commercial airlines, in New York, Chicago, Florida, and California, never understanding why, and always blaming his employers' stupidity or spite. After that, he failed to find another job in his chosen profession. He earned his living, or rather his drink, as best he could, taking whatever turned up. But wherever he went, there was always some warm tavern or bar to take refuge in. He stopped eating, his clothes deteriorated. Nothing mattered any more—street or gutter, it was all one—so long as he could get liquor, even of the worst quality.

One night in a bar he ceased to be aware of what he was doing, though without actually passing out. When he came to himself, he saw a friend who was a member of Alcoholics Anonymous sitting beside him.

"What are you doing here?" Bruce asked.

"You've just telephoned to ask me to help you join us," his friend said.

And when Bruce pictured himself staggering to the telephone booth like a sleepwalker, he realized that the appeal for help must have come from the depths of his being, without his conscious will having any part in it.

"And I've fought hard to keep sober ever since. I've got another regular job, and I'm learning how to begin life again," ended Bruce P.

His hands still gripped the stem of the microphone. His face was covered in sweat. He didn't seem to hear the applause which rose from the audience.

The speaker who came next seemed even younger, with his round face and his crew cut.

"My name is Wilbur K. and I'm an alcoholic," he said.

His parents were upper-class and very rich. He had never gone short of money, even as an adolescent. He developed an unbridled passion for drink while still very young, and his first fits of anxiety came to threaten him when he was eighteen. Since his parents lived in an exclusive suburb, they bought him a car to drive the fifteen miles to the university.

One evening when he got in, he became aware of a complete gap in his memory. He had absolutely no recollection of coming home. He looked for his car in front of the house, then in back; at last he found it in the garage. His first impulse was to see if there was blood on it, for he might easily have run someone down. His memory was entirely blank.

"In spite of this danger signal, I went on drinking more heavily than before, and every day I ran the risk of killing someone," said the fresh-faced young man with the crew cut and frank smile.

When he left the university, he got a very good job, thanks to his father, and did very well in it. He made a lot of money, traveling all the time in the greatest comfort at the firm's expense. But drink had got him, and it began to play havoc with his life. Slips and professional errors, harmless at first, grew more serious and more frequent. Wilbur's boss learned of his alcoholism and gave the young man a choice: he could stop drinking or leave the firm.

Wilbur made an effort to keep sober and succeeded for a while. Then, one day, when he was in San Francisco on business, he read a story in *The New Yorker*.

"I still don't understand what happened," said Wilbur K. in a surprised and thoughtful tone of voice that didn't seem natural to him. "There was nothing about drink or any other of my failings in that story. But as soon as I'd finished it I went on a binge."

He never knew how long it lasted, nor how he got back to New York. He had crossed the entire continent from one side to another, while blind drunk.

"After that," said Wilbur K., "I went on drinking for another year. And you can take it from me I was in danger of a worse fate than a mental institution or prison even."

However, it was in a prison cell that the young man was visited by a friend who was a member of Alcoholics Anonymous and who had often tried to get him to join his group. Wilbur had always refused; but this time he agreed.

"Now my boss has taken me back into the firm," he declared. "And everything's going fine. Too well; I'm putting on a lot of weight."

Laughter and cheers greeted this peroration.

Wilbur K. jumped lightly down from the platform,

◇◇◇

and an intermission of a few minutes was announced. The third and last speaker was to come after it. And what a speaker!

The intermission lasted some time, so as to allow a collection to be made. Each Rhinelander deposited his contribution in an aluminum plate.

The characterless white hall of the church, so brilliantly lit, so crowded with rich, smart people, once again seemed to be the scene of a fashionable evening party. But the stories these two young men had told of their wretched existences as alcoholics still echoed around the dazzling walls. I looked about for the speakers, but in vain. They were lost in the crowd.

"You noticed the difference between the two boys who spoke?" Bob asked me.

"Of course," I said. "It was torture to the first to have to expose himself before us all. And he still carries the marks of his disease. Whereas the second is in the best of health and appears quite at ease."

"Perhaps that's because Wilbur joined Alcoholics Anonymous before Bruce did," said Bob. "But the essential difference is in their temperaments. Some people give up drinking and transform their whole lives with astounding speed and ease. But for others, perhaps less affected by the poison, it's a long painful road, sprinkled with temptations, trials, and relapses."

Bob's smile was an admission of his own weakness, as he went on:

"For instance, take our friend Harry, who sent you to

me when you met him in Paris. He and I were drinking about even. Well, he went to his first Alcoholics Anonymous meetings as if they were parties, and after four of them everything was all right, it was finished. But I used to slip shamefacedly into the back row, and choose groups where I ran no risk of being recognized. And afterwards—the inner conflicts, the struggles I had to go through!"

A big bald man with a genial manner got up and tapped my companion on the shoulder.

"Hello, Bob!" he said beaming.

"Fred!" Bob said delightedly.

They talked about trivial matters, but with the warmest friendliness, and then parted company.

"He's a Wall Street broker," said Bob. "For years we used to meet in the same bar, both before and after work. We understood each other fine: he drank as much as I did. We kept in step. Then I began life afresh with Alcoholics Anonymous, and when I joined this group —who should I see at my first meeting but Fred? We certainly must have been tuned in on the same wave length."

Bob laughed heartily.

"Why did you change groups?" I asked. "All your friends seem to be in this one."

"That's true," said Bob. "But. . . ."

He glanced around the audience, and went on, smiling:

"But I've already told you that the Rhinelanders have been nicknamed the Mink and Sable group, because of their social standing. After a time I thought I'd rather join another. Understand?"

Before I had had time to answer, Bob said with feeling:

"It's not that the problem of drink is less serious, terrible, and tragic for the rich than for anyone else. Oh. far from it! But the rest have other problems as well.'

Bob's face had taken on the expression that at times made it so remarkably attractive. I think it was at this moment that my sympathy and gratitude turned into friendship.

A woman held out the collection plate to us and then made her way along our row of chairs. I watched her with pleasure. She was very young and charming and exquisitely dressed, with a fur stole round her long willowy neck. I had a sudden idea, which I immediately rejected as impossible.

"Of course that girl doesn't belong to Alcoholics Anonymous?" I asked Bob.

"She certainly does," said my companion. "I repeat: there's not a soul here who isn't an alcoholic."

"But she's so young!" I said. "It's unbelievable!"

Bob nodded.

"You know, there's a lot of drinking at women's universities, too. Like the boys, the girls have their societies, public or secret, whose members glory in getting intoxicated. So that any who are vulnerable to alcohol may become victims of it for life."

The young girl was still making her rounds.

"But nowadays young alcoholics get a chance they

◇◇◇

never had before," Bob went on. "Every year Alcoholics Anonymous are better known. The sooner they join, the less difficult it is for them."

The beautiful collector passed in front of us again. Her task was finished.

The leader of the meeting, the well-dressed cheerful publicity agent who had once been a hopeless drunkard, now stepped on to the platform again.

"Before we go on with the meeting," he said, "I have a piece of good news to announce which affects me personally."

He paused for a moment and then added:

"The directors of my firm have chosen me to handle a very important advertising contract: for Seagram's, the well-known whisky distillers. Not bad for a member of Alcoholics Anonymous, is it?—for they know I am one, all right."

There was a storm of laughter.

"Isn't he making light of something serious?" I asked Bob.

"It never does any harm to have a sense of humor," he said. "Especially in our case. It stops us from pitying ourselves. And self-pity leads straight to the bottle."

The leader made a gesture for silence.

"I shall now call upon the third and last member of my team," he said.

A woman came forward, a woman I shall never be able to forget. She was old, tall, bony, and respectably but very unfashionably dressed. Her skirt was long. Her thin neck, with the tendons standing out like cords emerged from the shallow V of her bodice. Her face was covered in fine, deep wrinkles, and her mouth never stopped quivering.

"My name is Kay S.," she said, "and I am an alcoholic."

The customary words fell from her lips with evident difficulty, almost pain. This was not because of any mental or moral constraint on her part. It was due to a physical infirmity. This woman had to struggle all the time against a muscular contraction of the throat. She had to force out each syllable with a desperate effort in spite of a stammer that contracted and convulsed her ascetic face.

In this grim manner she went through with her speech to the bitter end.

She came of a rich Irish family and had been brought up by an old nurse who treated the little girl's frequent colds with a well-sweetened drink made half of warm milk, half of whisky. The child got such a taste for her medicine that she feigned a cough so as to get it.

"To make a long story short, I was an alcoholic before I was ten years old," said Kay S.

Later on, she used to drink her father's liquor on the sly.

It was in the days of prohibition, and when she went to school she got her supplies from the boys, who made it a point of honor to get hold of illicit and sometimes deadly spirits. Then came the age of parties, and cocktail drinking to excess.

"When I married," said the old lady with trembling

lips, "I could have been—I ought to have been—happy. Everything combined to make me so. My husband was charming and kind. We had a fine house in California; children. But drink came first of all. I knew quite well that I was overdoing it, but I thought I could carry any quantity with dignity. After all, I came of a good family, didn't I? I was a *lady*."

The old lady spat out this word in a way that made me shiver; there was misery and sarcasm in it, and desperate self-mockery.

"We entertained and went out a great deal," continued Kay S. "When I was drunk I said cruel and wounding things, and there were scandalous scenes. What did it matter, I used to say smugly. After all I was a lady.

"My husband began to worry about it; he tried to reason with me, and grew angry. I took very little notice. He didn't understand me in the least. I was a lady.

"Then one of my daughters fell dangerously ill. I made a vow that I would stop drinking if she recovered. I got my wish. But I wasn't going to stop drinking for a little thing like that. As for my vow—I settled that by a form of self-trickery. My promise was about giving up drink, wasn't it? That was easy: I wouldn't—for a while—touch whisky; instead I would drink wine, quantities and quantities of it. Disgraceful . . . but can a lady behave disgracefully?"

The word was like an abominable refrain, changing its note from irony to bitterness, hatred, and self-loathing. And this old lady with the tendons of her neck

swollen like deformed plant stems, unmercifully scourg-
ing her own past and stammering out her public confession with implacable determination, had the noble
despair and eloquence of one of Shakespeare's characters. She even made use of the same turn of oratory
as Mark Antony against Brutus in *Julius Caesar*. But
Kay S.'s onslaught was directed against herself.

"My husband left me," she continued. "I had no family
and no money left. It was all the fault of others, never
mine. But then a real lady always shows her true metal
in misfortune, don't you think so?

"I drank like a lunatic; it didn't matter what. I used
to reel and stagger in the street, but if anyone helped
me stand upright I could always say thank you. Oh
yes! I was a lady.

"For lack of money I used to go to the most squalid
bars. But I always carried *The New York Times*
under my arm. It's a high-class paper, you see—the paper a lady should read.

"And when I was so sodden with drink that my lips
refused to move, when I felt the whole room revolving
and the world collapsing around the disheveled unwashed woman I had become, I used to open my *Times*
and 'read' it—even if I held it upside down, as I was
seen doing more than once. You know why? Because
I was a lady."

Repetition automatically produces a comic effect.
There was some laughter from the audience. This was
what the old woman on the platform wanted. She
wanted to subject the frightful shadow of herself that

she had summoned up to the castigation of general mockery. But the laughter was forced and nervous. It was painful to listen to.

Suddenly there was silence. Kay S. was saying:

"And I went on being a lady up till the moment when I found myself in a clinic for mental disorders. It wasn't only that I was mad, I was dumb as well. I couldn't utter a single word, or syllable even. They took care of me, they re-educated me. It was agony."

The old woman described every stage in her agony. And as she related how her lips, tongue, and throat re-learned the movements and sound of human speech, one felt that the memory of those ghastly weeks must paralyze her afresh, so great must be her pain in reviving it. But she obviously wanted to suffer all the stages of the torments she owed to her alcoholism, and to make her listeners suffer them, too. She didn't spare herself or her audience a single detail.

"I was cured—or very nearly," Kay S. went on. "And at the same time I knew that if I drank a single glass of liquor—in any shape or form—I would be lost for ever. So I approached Alcoholics Anonymous, and they advised, helped, and protected me. I owe them a debt that will only be paid with my last breath. And I will work for them to the end of my days."

There was a pregnant silence before the applause broke out. The faces around me wore a haunted expression.

The president of the group returned to the platform, and everyone got up. I did the same, without under-

◇◇◇

standing why, until I heard the first words of the
Common Prayer: "Our Father, which art in Heaven."

When it was over and the audience was slowly moving in the direction of the magnificent ultramodern
kitchen for coffee and cake, I said to Bob:

"I thought you assured me that Alcoholics Anonymous was in no sense a religious body. . . ."

"It isn't," he said. "You'll find people of all faiths
among us, as well as agnostics and atheists. The prayer,
you mean? Those who feel the need of it join in, and
the rest abstain. That's all there is to it."

"You're a journalist like me, Bob," I persisted. "And
you must see that when I tell how your meetings
end, people may easily think that your association is
a sort of Salvation Army—though personally I'm
beginning to realize its importance and remarkable
originality."

Bob laughed and replied:

"Lots of people over here get the same idea. That
doesn't matter in the least. But the results do."

I thought of the two young men who had spoken, the
pretty girl who had taken up the collection, the president of the Rhinelanders, the leader of the meeting, and
above all, above all I thought of Kay, the stammering
old lady.

"But how do they get their results?" I wanted to know.

At that moment we were approached by a tall
woman of about forty-five, whose fine face was so full
of simple nobility, tranquil suffering, and forceful personality that it reminded me of a classical mask.

◇◇◇

"Here's Eve M.," said Bob. "She's responsible for public relations for Alcoholics Anonymous. Ask her."

"Come to our office after lunch tomorrow," said the tall woman with the expressive eyes. "Bill W. will be there. He was the founder of Alcoholics Anonymous."

VI

A. A.

My taxi put me down opposite 141 East 44th Street, close to Great Central Station. The street was poor and shabby looking, and there were metal fire escapes fixed to the dreary façades. The houses were not very tall, and installed in them were various small businesses in keeping with the neighborhood, the inhabitants, and the passers-by, such as fruit stands, dyers, cafeterias, and snack bars.

No. 141 was an office building ten stories high, just as drab as the rest. On the wall of the aisle-like hall was a board showing the names of all the firms lodged in the building. I at once saw what I was looking for:

ALCOHOLICS ANONYMOUS
General Service Office
SECOND FLOOR

◇◇

I stood in front of this notice for a few seconds, feeling strangely anxious. What would I find on the second floor? Invalids or saints?

Certainly Harry X., Bob N., and the few other Alcoholics Anonymous I had met had been neither. On the contrary, they were simple, humane, intelligent, sensitive people who had immediately aroused my admiration and friendship. But they were only ordinary members, they held no official position or rank. Whereas up above. . . .

Up above I should find people whose sole business and function it was to live by and for the movement, enthusiasts and professionals at the same time. And among them I was to meet the man who had conceived the idea of Alcoholics Anonymous and brought it to life. Would he be a fanatic, an ascetic, a preacher, or the founder of a sect?

I pulled myself together and entered the antiquated, shabby elevator.

"Second floor," I said to the elevator operator hurriedly and with a ridiculous feeling of embarrassment.

I couldn't help reflecting that this tired, surly man knew the place I was going to better than anyone, and must certainly take me for "one of them."

He made no comment and left me, without so much as a glance, in a narrow corridor in front of the door of Alcoholics Anonymous.

I pushed it open and found myself in an office like that of any moderate-sized business. There was a switchboard operator on the left, a typist on the right. The switchboard operator was fat and jolly; the secretary, slim and charming.

The secretary asked me the usual question:

"Can I help you?"

I told her I had an appointment with Eve M. The girl plugged in a line, gave my name, and then told me that Miss M. was sorry that she must ask me to wait a few minutes. She still had with her the delegates of a Western state, who had come to New York on the association's business.

I sat down on a metal chair, with my back against a metal filing cabinet (the room was rather cluttered), and cast my eye over the leaflets and papers lying close at hand.

The first thing that struck me was that the association was always referred to by its initials, A. A., as if everyone had heard of it. In my conversations with Bob I had often heard him use the abbreviation, and I had supposed that it was part of the initiates' vocabulary, a sort of group slang. But the format, lightness, and lack of bulk of the literature I was studying proved that it was intended for very wide distribution among a public still ignorant and in need of education and enlightenment.

I remember some of the titles:

Young People and A. A.
An Introduction to A. A.
Is A. A. for You?
A. A. Tradition: How it Developed
A. A. and the Medical Profession

◇◇◇

I also remember my growing uneasiness as I ran my eyes over these titles and others like them. In spite of Bob's protestations and example, I felt I was in a center of proselytism, among people suffering from some strange disease, who had reached a position halfway between past drunkenness and fanatical confidence.

Now and again—to bring myself back to earth—I watched the two girls in the office. The switchboard operator was handling a call; the typist tapped away at her machine. They were ordinary, normal office workers.

But these reflections were interrupted by the appearance of Eve M., the woman I had come to see, in the doorway that led to the main corridor of the A. A. premises.

Since I had met her for a moment at the gathering the night before, her forceful noble face was already known to me. But now that I saw her away from the crowd, with her tall distinguished silhouette framed between the two walls, and her serious, generous face deeply etched by the sorrows of life, she impressed me even more.

"Do forgive me for being late; I couldn't help it," she said in a slightly husky but musical and attractive voice. "Now I'm entirely at your service."

Nothing could possibly have been more banal. But there was something extraordinarily welcoming in the dignified and friendly way it was said. It had been just the same—I suddenly remembered—with Harry X.

and Bob. But in their cases I had put it down to the fact that we belong to the same profession, whereas this time I was confronted with a foreign woman, no longer young, who was receiving me in her official capacity only.

I followed Eve M. into her office. It was clean, simple, almost austere, furnished solely with a view to work, littered with graphs, memoranda, loose and filed documents, letters awaiting signature—in short, a business office in full swing.

There were several large maps spread on the walls.

"Please don't hesitate to tell me what you wish to know and to see," said Eve M. "We'll give you all the information we can."

But at this moment one of the telephones began to ring, and then a second. A secretary came in to ask for instructions. The telephones began ringing again. Another secretary appeared.

Eve M. answered all the questions and dealt with everything quickly and clearly, with precision and authority, and also in a quiet gentle manner that made her performance doubly effective. She was the embodiment of practical intelligence and organizing power.

At last there was a lull.

"Now I can give you all my attention," said Eve M., and her smile seemed to light up her serious face from within.

I couldn't resist the curiosity that had been aroused in me by her inexhaustible energy and an administrative skill that would have done credit to the manager of a large business.

"Were you once . . . ," I began, and stopped, suddenly embarrassed by the word I was going to say. But Eve M. had already finished my sentence for me.

"An alcoholic?" she said, looking me straight in the eye.

She smiled again, but this time her firmly cut lips twisted a little.

"Certainly I was," she went on. "And so horribly far gone that except for A. A. I should be dead or locked up by now."

She was still gazing at me steadily. I asked her the first question that came into my head.

"Are you a volunteer worker here?"

Eve M. shook her head gently.

"No," she said. "I get a salary. Most A. A. members give their time freely to the association or to other alcoholics, as you know. But that means such time as they can spare from their ordinary tasks or careers. I am one of the very few whose jobs involve giving up all other activities. My work is the one thing I live for."

"From the little I've seen, you're never short of it," I said.

"No, thank heaven!" Eve M. exclaimed. "The association is spreading further every day."

"Where to?" I asked.

"Come and see," said Eve M.

She took me to the maps hung on the wall; they

showed both hemispheres. At first I couldn't believe my eyes. Did those little squares full of letters and numbers in every continent and every country really stand for. . . .

"Yes, there are A. A.'s all over the world," Eve M. replied in answer to my unspoken question.

I went closer and studied the maps more carefully. It was fantastic: there wasn't a single country (except those of the Communist bloc, of course) without its A. A. sign, from north to south and from east to west of the terrestrial globe.

There was infinite variation in the density of the rectangles. In North America they were packed as closely as the cells of a honeycomb. Elsewhere they looked quite lost in space. All the same, a few were to be found everywhere, from Bechuanaland in Africa to the Ryukyu Islands off Japan.

I wouldn't like to say how long I stood silent in front of those maps. Minutes or seconds—what does it matter? It was long enough for me to realize what Alcoholics Anonymous stood for in terms of human solidarity and sheer size.

"What's the meaning of the letters *M*, *G*, and *L* in each rectangle?" I asked Eve M.

"*M* is membership—number of members," she said. "*G*—number of local groups. *L* stands for lone members."

I put my finger on the part of the map representing Mozambique. "Then where we see the figure one for number of members and also for lone members, I sup-

◇◇

pose both figures refer to the same person?" I said.

"Yes," said Eve M. "The same. The only one. But he's linked with all his friends by hope."

I gazed at the map and thought about this solitary individual whose existence had been sufficiently ruined by alcohol for him to join A. A., and who was now out there under the fierce tropical sun, struggling against temptation, delirium, and madness. He was physically alone and socially alone; if he had been morally alone as well, he would certainly have given in to his terrible craving. But between the monster and himself stood all the people represented by the other little rectangles on the map. There was Harry X., there was Bob. There was John M. And this woman with the noble tormented face beside me.

I began to understand.

"How many are there of you in the whole world?" I asked quietly.

"About three hundred thousand. But most are in the United States," said Eve M.

She took a fairly large pale blue book and a small leaflet with a bright yellow cover from the table. The title of the first was World Yearbook, Spring 1959. It contained the names of all the groups of A. A. in the five continents. There were two hundred and seventy large pages of close print. The other listed all the weekly meetings held by New York groups. There were nearly five hundred.

I was reduced to silence again.

"But all that is only a drop in the ocean," went on

Eve M. "It's estimated that in the United States alone the number of alcoholics is between *five and six million*. I'm not talking about people who drink regularly and only get drunk now and again, but about those to whom alcohol is a problem, to use our own phrase. As you see, the field is a vast one."

"When was the movement started?" I asked.

"Just twenty-five years ago," Eve M. told me.

"By whom? Where? How?"

Eve M. glanced at her wrist watch.

"Bill should be there now," she said. "Come along. He was the one who began it all."

VII

The Meeting at Akron

"So I'm going to see Bill W.," I reflected as I followed Eve M., public relations officer to Alcoholics Anonymous (or A. A., as I now began to call it, like everyone else). "I'm going to see the creator of this extraordinary association founded on despair and recovery, with a membership of hundreds of thousands spread into the remotest corners of the world."

And once again, as I walked along the corridor past the various offices of A. A. headquarters (each occupied by an ex-alcoholic whole sole purpose in life was to re-animate those who had become zombies through drink) —once again I wondered anxiously what Bill W. would be like. A deluded old man? A senile dreamer? A bombastic and fanatical prophet? A fervent theorist? The high priest of some dogma?

Never did an imaginary portrait turn out so inaccurate.

In a barely furnished small room devoid of papers I

◇◇◇

found a large loose-limbed man, not more than sixty
years old, wonderfully approachable, wonderfully alert
in mind and body, and wonderfully friendly. Under his
short crop of white hair, his lean face was full of energy, youth, intelligence, and humor; it was one of
those peculiarly American faces which after a certain
age suggest both a Roman senator and a successful
businessman. In addition, it was attractively asym-
metrical, with narrow eyes that sparkled all the time
with gaiety and kindly irony.

He knew why I had come. And without preamble or
the slightest self-consciousness he began telling me one
of the most staggering human histories I have ever
heard, as if he were talking about somebody else's very
ordinary experiences.

I shall set it down in full. Not only is it the story of a
most astonishing life, but it also reveals how widely
the terrible curse of alcoholism has spread through the
United States, to what depths it has penetrated, and the
peculiar and sometimes incredible forms it takes in the
men and women of this country.

Bill W. didn't touch his first glass of liquor till he was
twenty-one and had got his commission during the First
World War.

Born in Vermont, one of the oldest, most puritan,
and Yankee of North American states, he had been
brought up with patriarchal tenderness by his parents
and grandparents in a village of fifty houses. Afterwards
he went to boarding school, where he easily outdid

◇◇◇

the other boys in class after class, thus fulfilling the longing for power and priority that had obsessed him from early childhood.

In fact, his childhood and adolescence were normal or even privileged, except at moments when his basic, passionate desire for pre-eminence was wounded or frustrated.

When the United States came into the war in 1917, Bill W. joined the Officers' Training Corps. At the same moment he fell in love with a girl who returned his love, and married her.

Here he was, then, married to a young woman he adored and who adored him, a tall, slim, handsome second lieutenant, proud of his rank and his new uniform. Fate seemed to have produced one of those rare combinations of circumstances that create a perfect moment in life, like a delightful oasis.

But his obsession to do better than other ordinary mortals would not leave him in peace. Now, just because of his rank and his uniform and his charming wife, he was invited to the richest and most exclusive houses in the town where his regiment was stationed. In them he was confronted by a way of life that he had never dreamed existed. He saw a butler for the first time. He was paralyzed by his dread of appearing inferior to these people—he, who had always wanted to come first and do better than anyone. He suddenly found himself unable to string two sentences together, two words even. . . .

One evening when he was in the grip of this recur-

ring anxiety, someone gave him a Bronx cocktail, and
he swallowed his first glass of alcoholic liquor without
knowing what he was drinking. His timidity, fear, and
humiliation vanished immediately. He held forth; he
shone. Another cocktail and yet another, and he was
the success of the party. Drink had shown him the way
to make contact with other men, however rich and ex-
alted they might be.

By the time Bill W. embarked for France and the
front, drink was a delightful habit to him. But it grew
upon him to a disastrous extent under the influence
of the rough comradeship of active service and the dissi-
pations of leave.

When he got back to the United States, Bill W. was
consumed with impatience to make a lot of money, and
through money to achieve power. He felt he had an absolute right to it, that it was his destiny. At twenty-two,
wasn't he already a veteran of a glorious campaign?
Hadn't he already been a leader and master of men, for
whose life or death he was responsible?

But the only job he could find was that of clerk to a
railway company.

He showed so little enthusiasm for it that he soon
was fired. He moved on to Wall Street. It was a period of
wild speculation and boom; huge fortunes were being
made through flair or luck. He had an immediate, triumphant success.

Bill was drinking more and more, steadily, day and
night. That didn't trouble him. When his wife Lois wor-
ried about it, he said to her in all good faith:

"Men of genius always get their best inspiration when they're drunk."

Of course, there was a certain amount of talk from time to time. Some people who had admired and been fond of him began to avoid him, and painful scenes took place in his luxurious flat. What did it matter? Young as he was, Bill went on handling millions of dollars and frequenting the best restaurants and the smartest society. And in that period of frenzied jazz, when prohibition was falling into utter contempt, he went on drinking, drinking, drinking.

In October 1929 the most terrible crisis the United States had ever known struck Wall Street like a cyclone, and the golden columns of the temple toppled and fell. Bill W. heard the news while he was staying at one of the best known, most exclusive country clubs. Dressed in the latest fashion in a suède coat, he was more often to be seen in the bar than on the green. He was told that he had lost every penny he possessed and a good deal more; and that rich speculators and stockbrokers whom he saw every day had killed themselves rather than face total ruin.

He went straight to the bar and stayed there till he had had as many drinks as he needed. When he left, he had got back all his confidence. He wasn't the sort of man to jump out of a twentieth or thirtieth story over a little thing like that. He was made of sterner stuff. He would find a way out. They would soon see.

As it happened, thanks to a friend in Montreal who had managed to hang on to a considerable part of his capital, he was able to carry on for another year without altering his way of life. But his alcoholic intake had reached a disastrous point; he could neither control nor conceal his drinking bouts. His friend in Montreal withdrew his help.

Bill and Lois were soon in serious difficulties. They had to give up their luxurious apartment and take refuge in a humble house in Brooklyn belonging to Lois's parents. Bill made the long trip to Wall Street by subway, but he was only an encumbrance now, a parasite, a shadow of his former self. It was Lois who kept the household going; she found a job as saleswoman in a Brooklyn department store.

Nothing of what had once made life valuable was left to Bill—nothing except drink, and even that had ceased to have a tonic effect or inspire dreams of power and glory. It had acquired a new, simpler, sadder function: to deaden his misery. And instead of subtly mixed cocktails, he was now drinking three or four bottles a day of acrid brownish gin, which he brewed himself in his bathtub.

But his luck had not entirely deserted him. At the height of the economic crisis, a large financial undertaking suddenly offered him a job that seemed likely to bring him millions of dollars. Bill's old pride, his old longing for pre-eminence was aroused. It was obvious that he wasn't the sort of man who could let his wife keep him by working in a store. This time he was sure to make his fortune. There was, however, one special clause in the agreement: while the contract lasted—

and that was a long time—he must undertake not to drink.

He signed cheerfully. He was responsible for his own actions, wasn't he?

A contract is a solemn, almost sacred thing to the Yankees of Vermont. Bill kept scrupulously sober for three months.

At last the project he was involved in got underway. He went to look at a possible factory site a long way from New York. One evening he was in his hotel talking to several engineers, when a jug of spirits was passed around the table. Bill remembered his contract and thought of Lois, and when his turn came he was gratified by the ease with which he found himself saying: "No, thanks." But the conversation went on and on. He grew bored. The jug was still going its rounds. And someone said:

"You know, Bill, this is the strongest applejack there is—Jersey lightning. And there's not much of it left."

Then it suddenly came into Bill's head that he had never in all his drinking career had a chance of tasting Jersey lightning.

"You're right," he said, "a little drop can't do me any harm."

He swallowed the "little drop," and immediately Lois and the clause in the contract ceased to exist for him. His old obsession reigned supreme, awakened by the applejack.

Then followed a gap in his consciousness, a complete blank, a blackout—and it lasted three days.

After he came to himself, Bill got a telephone call informing him that his contract was canceled—and his wealth and security gone.

The next two years were years of self-created hell for Bill W. He experienced all the delusions, torments, and humiliations of an alcoholic with his back to the wall. There were shameful requests for loans, unpaid debts to tradesmen, bottles hidden all over the apartment, appalling hangovers, unspeakable terror and isolation when dawn came. Before he could touch his breakfast, he had to drink either a tumbler of gin or at least half a dozen bottles of beer. To pay for his drink he had gone as far as to rifle his wife's bag and steal some of the pitiable wages she earned at the store.

He reached the point of having to avoid looking at the medicine chest because it contained poison, and of sleeping on a mattress on the floor so as not to see the window, because he longed to throw himself out of it.

His brother-in-law, who was a doctor, tried to cure him with sedatives. But Bill mixed them with his gin, and nearly drove himself insane. He had to be taken in an ambulance to a clinic for mental disorders. From that moment, he was caught up in the infernal rhythm of so many alcoholics' lives: mental home, short period of abstinence, relapse, mental home. . . .

And it was in a mental home that he again found himself in September 1934.

He had become as thin as a skeleton. His nerves and his brain had been disordered to the breaking point. The exceptionally kind medical officer of the clinic, Dr.

Silkworth, felt obliged to warn Bill W.'s wife that he must soon die either of general debility or of softening of the brain, if he didn't give up drink entirely.

When Bill W. left the mental home, his wife passed on this warning to him. Bill knew that the kind white-haired doctor was a friend, and he trusted his verdict. Fear gave him the courage to abstain.

His appetite came back; he slept better. His physical and mental energy returned. He even succeeded in earning a few dollars here and there. And when he saw anxiety give place to timid, incredulous happiness in the weary face of his wife (who still worked to earn their living), he felt certain that never, never again, could he give way to that damnable temptation.

He even got into the habit of explaining his refusal of a glass of wine by means of a lecture on the ill effects of drink and its deadly dangers to him.

September passed in this way. October also.

On November 11, Bill had nothing to do. Because it was Armistice Day, there were no operations on Wall Street. But the Brooklyn department store stayed open, and Lois had to go to work as usual. Bill W. decided to go and play golf, and, as there was little money to spare, he chose Staten Island, where the links were open to the public.

When he told his wife, he saw a shadow of the old uneasiness cross her face, but she got the better of her anxiety and said cheerfully:

"You're quite right. It'll do you good."

In the bus, Bill W. got to talking to another passenger, who was carrying a rifle. He was also taking advantage of the holiday to go to Staten Island, but to the rifle range.

There was an inn at the bus terminal, and it was lunch time. The two travelers sat down at the same table.

"A whisky," said the man with the rifle.

"Lemonade," said Bill.

Then he told his companion the disastrous effect alcohol had on him.

Just as he had finished, the bartender, a huge Irishman with a beaming face, came up to them with a glass in each hand.

"On the house, boys!" he cried. "It's Armistice Day!"

Everything else vanished from Bill's mind except the memory of November 11, 1918, in France, and the wild joy and festivities of that triumphant day. Without hesitating for a moment, he took the glass and swallowed its contents.

"After what you've just told me! You must be mad!" cried his companion.

"I am," said Bill.

Then came utter darkness.

At five o'clock next morning, Lois found her husband lying unconscious in front of their house. He had struck the iron railing as he fell, and his scalp was bleeding freely. His hand clutched the handle of his bag of golf clubs.

When Bill came round, Lois and he said very little to

◇◇

each other. There was nothing to say. The situation had never before been so desperate for them. Bill started making his own gin in the bathtub again, one, two, three bottles a day. He couldn't stop, and he knew it.

He didn't go to Wall Street anymore. What was the use? The dreams of wealth, power, and glory that had so often acted as a spur were dead now. The slump would pass. Wall Street would be its old self again; there would be a new wave of prosperity. But he would have no part in it. He was a lost, doomed soul.

One gloomy November evening, Bill W., not yet forty years old, was down in the basement kitchen of the old Brooklyn house lent him by his wife's parents and now mortgaged to the limit. He was alone. Lois hadn't yet come home from the store, where she still earned the wages that kept them alive.

On the table in front of Bill stood a large bowl full of gin mixed with a small quantity of pineapple juice to improve the taste. Bill stared at this murky brew and remembered the days when he had been a dazzling success on Wall Street, when he was young, enthusiastic, strong, and rich and the world had been at his feet. Drink had swallowed up everything. He had tried to fight against it. In vain. It was all over for him now. There was nothing to be done. He would soon be dead, as gentle wise Dr. Silkworth, who had many times cared for him in his mental clinic, had predicted. Poor Lois. Poor Bill. . . .

He refilled his glass automatically. What was the use

of measuring the dose, once you had reached the depths of despair and the end of your life? He only wanted the bludgeon to knock him senseless quickly, quickly. Oh yes, of course there would be a horrible awakening, fear, and misery in the dawn. That couldn't be helped. It was the present moment that mattered. Bill reached out his hand toward his deadly solace.

He was interrupted by the ringing of the telephone. He went to answer it automatically, but without the faintest curiosity. He was not expecting a call from any-one. Suddenly a feeling of intense pleasure over-whelmed him. It was Ebby, a friend of his youth who like him had become entirely addicted to drink. What marvelous, crazy sprees they had been on together. Once they had even hired an airplane (both of them completely drunk) so as to continue their glorious drinking bout two thousand miles away. Ebby was rich, and he had gone off to drink in Europe. A year ago Bill had heard that he had been shut up in a mental home. So he must have come out and remembered Bill and thought he'd come and drink with him. . . .

How delightful! He wouldn't be alone any more. They would talk about the good old days, and get drunk together. . . .

"Come alone, come right away!" cried Bill into the receiver. "I've got everything here. I'll be ready for you."

And here was Ebby now in the kitchen. Bill hurried forward to greet him—then he stopped.

He saw Ebby's eyes. They were clear, intelligent, and shining. They weren't the eyes of a drunk at all.

Bill was sure of that. What he had been through made him sure of it. Ebby, Ebby the most abandoned, frenzied drunk he had ever known, his unfailing companion on innumerable unbridled drinking bouts, was sober—and had been sober for a long time.

All the same Bill made one desperate effort: he pushed the bowl of gin towards his former drinking companion.

"Thanks, but I don't drink any more," said Ebby with a friendly smile.

"But what's happened to you?" cried Bill.

"I've found another purpose in life," said Ebby: "faith."

"Oh, I see," said Bill.

He was in fact reassured by this answer. The mental home had taken Ebby in as an alcoholic maniac, and he had come out a religious one. That was very easy to understand.

"I see, I see," Bill repeated.

"No, it's not that at all. I'm not nuts," said Ebby laughing quietly. "I'll tell you what happened. A friend of mine, as thorough an alcoholic as I was, consulted the great Swiss psychoanalyst, Carl Jung. His diagnosis was: incurable alcoholism which must soon end fatally. But he added that what medicine and psychiatry could not do was sometimes achieved by a violent emotional shock or spiritual revelation. This was the only hope, and Jung hadn't much belief in it.

"Well, it happened to my friend, and he shared it with me."

◇◇◇

"What brand of religion is it?" asked Bill sarcastically.

"Oh, I don't think it has a special name," said Ebby gaily. "It's the Oxford Group I'm talking about. Without accepting all their ideas—very far from it—I did learn some essential things. For instance, to accept the fact that I was down and out, done for, liquidated. To sum up my own character and confide all my faults to another person; to put right any wrongs I might have perpetrated; and, above all, to make a present of myself to other people. . . ."

Bill tried to speak, but his friend stopped him.

"I know you're going to laugh at me, but I shall finish my story all the same. That's what I came here for. These people also taught me that if I wanted to have the strength to carry out these precepts, I must pray to God. But that this God need not conform to the pattern handed down for centuries, that I was free to conceive of him as I wished, and that if I didn't believe in any God at all (even in so wide a sense), I must try to pray to a God who might exist to give me the courage I needed.

"Then something very strange happened—before I had even made the attempt, simply as a result of resolving to do so to the best of my ability. I was suddenly relieved of my craving for drink. It wasn't just one of those times you and I know so well, when you force yourself to be sober and yet are still haunted by the old obsession. No, I hadn't the smallest desire for drink. And that has lasted for months now. . . ."

After Ebby had gone, Bill drank like a madman for several days.

It was true that as a child he had been brought up in the puritan tradition of the old country. But later on his scientific studies and the years on Wall Street had made him a rationalist and an extreme materialist.

However, during the few intervals of lucidity his drinking left him, Bill kept thinking of what his friend had said. Ebby hadn't behaved like a preacher or a moralist. He hadn't put any pressure on him. He was simply *one alcoholic talking to another.*

Perhaps there was something in this idea of God, after all. . . .

In order to clear up the matter, Bill went to Calvary Church where some members of the Oxford Group had managed to find a room for Ebby. It was a long way from Brooklyn, and there were plenty of bars along the road. Bill arrived very drunk, with his arm around a Finnish sailmaker whom he had picked up on the way.

The Oxford Group had opened a mission in Calvary House for the benefit of every sort of human wreck. Most of them were alcoholics. The meeting room stank of stale sweat and of the whisky, gin, beer, and the worst quality wine with which their breaths were impregnated.

Bill had never been in such company before. But his intoxicated state led him to take a sleepwalker's part in all the prayers of repentance, fall on his knees, and make a fiery speech of which he could never afterwards

◇◇

recall a single word. Then he went with Ebby to the dormitory. There he found some alcoholics who had been restored to sobriety and health. They lived in the mission and worked in the neighborhood all day. Listening to their talk soon had a sobering effect on Bill. He thought of Lois. It was night now, and she must be anxious. He hurriedly telephoned her and took the subway home.

As he went down the steps, he noticed that he hadn't even thought of stopping in a bar. Why not? He was aware of a vague but immense feeling of hope.

This hope inspired every word of the conversation Bill had with Lois that night, and he fell asleep as soundly as a child, without a drop of his usual soporific —gin.

He awoke just before dawn, feeling anxious. And he said to himself that a glass—only one small glass, or maybe two—would enable him to see the sunrise with pleasure.

Lois was asleep. Bill got up quietly, swallowed his ration, and rinsed his mouth with mouthwash. Lois noticed nothing. She went off to work, and Bill was alone. His chronic craving became urgent. When Lois got home, she found Bill lying on his bed, dead drunk.

The bout went on for three days. But all through it, Ebby's sermon kept returning to his semiconscious mind, now stupefied, now excited by alcohol. Finally Bill said to himself:

"This is my last chance, but if I am to take it I must be

able to see clearly into my own mind. The only way is to take another cure and be 'disintoxicated.' "

Next morning Bill W. set off once more to the clinic where Dr. Silkworth had so often treated him. As he was leaving the house, he felt in his pockets. He had just six cents. He was reassured. A subway ride to the mental home cost five. . . .

But nothing could be bought with the remaining cent. Now Bill was subject to the special form of logic common to alcoholics about to begin a cure: he wanted a good drink before he arrived at the clinic. He remembered a grocer in the neighborhood with whom he still had some credit. He asked if he could let him have four bottles of beer on account, and the grocer was ready to oblige.

He swallowed the first bottle there and then, standing on the pavement, and the second in the subway. He was now getting more and more generous and friendly, and he offered the next to a man sitting near him. The offer was declined, so Bill emptied this third bottle on the platform of the station when he got out of the subway. He was holding the fourth by the neck as he entered the mental home.

Dr. Silkworth was waiting for him. Bill greeted him by brandishing his last bottle in the air and shouting:

"Doc, I've made a discovery at last."

In spite of the mists dancing before his eyes, Bill saw a look of unhappiness and pain cross the doctor's face. He was fond of this semilunatic and was sorry for him.

<><><><><><><><><><><><><><><><><><><><><><><><><><><><><><><>

When Bill tried to explain his discovery, the doctor shook his head and said gently:

"Come on, it's high time we put you to bed."

The cure took effect quickly. After four days the physical craving for alcohol had gone and the numbed stupefaction caused by the sedatives had worn off. But Bill was left in a state of deep moral depression. The fact that it was a beautiful morning made life all the more intolerable to him.

The door opened and in came Ebby, fresh and smiling. Bill found his high spirits exasperating. He felt a momentary suspicion that Ebby had come to preach to him. But Ebby only smiled and said nothing.

"Well?" Bill asked sarcastically. "Aren't you going to begin telling me your precious solution to all our problems again?"

Without losing any of his good humor, Ebby placidly stated the conditions necessary to recovery:

To admit utter defeat.

To be entirely honest with yourself.

To confess your weaknesses to someone else.

To make amends for any harm you may have done.

To try and give of your best without hope of reward.

To pray to God, however you may conceive of Him, if necessary simply as an experiment.

They talked about unimportant subjects, and Ebby said good-by to his friend.

Then something happened in that whitewashed room quite unimaginable to people like me, who have never practiced any religion or experienced anything approaching a sense of revelation or mystical illumination. That is why I propose to repeat word for word Bill W.'s own description of this extraordinary moment, just as he told it to me and as he also described it on paper.

"After Ebby went, my depression grew worse every moment till it was quite unbearable. It seemed to me I had reached rock bottom. I was still putting up a struggle against the notion of a Power greater than myself. But in the end, just for a second, my stubborn pride was broken. And I suddenly heard myself cry out:

" 'If there is a God, let Him show Himself! I'm ready for anything, anything.'

"Then, all at once, my room was filled with a great white light. No words can describe the ecstasy I felt. It seemed to me that I was on the top of a high mountain and that the wind that blew over it was not of air but of the spirit. And the conviction burst upon me that I was saved.

"Slowly my feeling of ecstasy grew quieter. But I had a wonderful awareness of a Presence all around me and pervading me, and I said to myself: 'So this is the God of the preachers!' "

Then Bill W. was gradually overtaken by intense fear. The abnormal emotional state he had just experienced—his initiation into the supernatural—was deeply disturbing to his logical mind. Was such a thing really possible and credible?

Bill remembered his condition when he arrived at the

mental home; how he had been weaned from drink; the calming drugs he had taken. Perhaps all this had finally unhinged his brain? Perhaps his ecstasy was only hallucination? The sense of the divine presence— lunacy?

Unable to bear this mental torment another instant, he sent an urgent summons to Dr. Silkworth, and explained his fears to him. The doctor questioned him for a long time, patiently and wisely. Then he said pensively:

"No, Bill, you're not mad. You've suffered some profound psychological or spiritual shock. I've read about such things. They sometimes save people from alcoholism."

Bill W. fell back on his pillow with a feeling of deep relief. Now he could reflect peacefully about this revelation, which had come to him like a miraculous flash of lightning.

When he left the mental home, his addiction to alcohol had no more power over him, old and deep though it was. He didn't even have to fight against its grip. The insatiable longing had gone. The insidious, noisy, secret summons was silent.

Drink was still the focus of Bill's life; but now he brought that same tenacity with which he once served the monster to the task of rescuing others. He had found the key to the problem: it lay in the fact that one alcoholic (in other words, Ebby) had spoken to another alcoholic (in other words, himself) about their common trouble. He only had to pass on this message, and he could snatch miserable wretches out of their self-made hell to safety.

Bill joined the Oxford Group's mission in the Calvary Church. He exerted all his enthusiasm and energy there. He tackled drunks and the other human wrecks in the dormitory, one after another. He had no success whatever. He even noticed that the alcoholics who had shown signs of wanting to abstain before he had experienced his revelation now fell back into the gulf.

Yet Bill persisted—partly because he was made that way, but even more because some fundamental instinct told him that by trying to help others he was first and foremost helping himself. The sight of utter ruin such as he had once experienced himself, and his crusade to rescue other sufferers formed a double line of defense. It was when he was talking to his brother alcoholics that Bill felt most invulnerable to alcohol.

He spent six months entirely occupied in this missionary activity. He talked to hundreds and hundreds of drunks. Not one of them gave up drinking.

Meanwhile, Lois was still wearing herself out earning a living for both of them. Bill made up his mind to see whether he couldn't make some money on Wall Street. He soon had an opportunity, and he left for Akron, an industrial town in Ohio, to negotiate for the purchase of a small factory there.

The transactions dragged on. Bill found himself alone with ten dollars in his pocket in the lobby of his hotel. He began to pace up and down. What was he to do?

Each time his automatic pacing brought him to the end of the hall that led into the bar, he became aware of the familiar, stimulating sounds: the chink of glasses, the liquid note of drinks being poured, the shaking-up of cocktails, warm voices, loud laughter. All this made up a sort of magic by which solitude could be exorcised. And Bill said to himself:

"I'll have a lemonade or a Coca-Cola."

He put out his hand, took hold of the doorknob—and didn't turn it. He suddenly remembered the countless times he had gone into a place where drinks were served, sober and firmly intending to remain so, and the appalling state he had been in when he left. Of course, he had experienced his revelation since then and passed six months without the ghost of a desire for a glass of liquor. But how could he tell what might happen when he found himself quite alone among cheerful drinkers, in an unknown town, with fifteen years of desperate alcoholism in the marrow of his bones? Bill shuddered. A relapse just now would be more frightful than any of the others, because it would mean the frustration of all his hopes.

Once again Bill started pacing up and down the hall of the hotel in Akron where fate had landed him. But this time he walked in dread. Now that he had realized the danger and *felt afraid* of it, it seemed to him that he had become vulnerable to the devilish temptation, and might give way to it. . . .

He concentrated his thoughts on a single point: how and why had he managed to get through six months without the smallest desire to drink? Mainly, of course, because of his religious experience. But in terms of practical, daily life? He suddenly knew the answer. He had found it easy to abstain because he had been trying to restore other alcoholics to sobriety all the time. By trying to help them, he had saved himself.

Yes, that was it; that alone would do: he must find an alcoholic at once and talk to him about his tragic addiction. But not one of the hotel visitors in the bar, a passer-by, a mere dabbler. No. Someone who was seriously ill, a chronic alcoholic with intoxication in his very bones, whose family life, profession, health, and self-esteem had all been affected by his disease. Yes, it was perfectly plain, he *needed* a man of that description. But how was he to find him in a town where he knew no one?

Bill's feverish gaze wandered around the hall and fell on a small table on which lay a leaflet containing the telephone numbers of various churches and clergymen in Akron. He snatched it up, opened it at random, and put through a call to the first name he saw: the Reverend Walter Tunks.

The Episcopalian clergyman listened to Bill W.'s entreaties in amazement. This unknown person talked in such a frantic hurry and so confusedly that the worthy parson thought he was being asked to find someone for Bill to get drunk with. In the end he understood what was wanted and gave him a list of ten people who might help him in his search.

Bill at once started calling them up. But it was Satur-

day afternoon. No one was home. Those who were were
sorry, they hadn't time. His list was nearly exhausted.
Soon there was only one telephone number left: that of
Mrs. Henrietta Seiberling.

He hesitated. The name was vaguely familiar to him.
Then he remembered that at the height of his success on
Wall Street he had met an old Mr. Seiberling, founder
and president of an enormous rubber company. Bill
tried for a moment to imagine the wife of this very important financier listening to an alcoholic asking for the
address of another alcoholic, for both their sakes—and
left the telephone booth.

Back in the hall, he resumed his pacing from one
end of the hall to the other. It was getting late. The
buzz of voices from the bar was growing louder
and more lively. Bill W. gritted his teeth, went back
to the telephone, and dialed the last number on his
list.

He heard a young and attractive voice speaking
with a southern accent.

Yes, it was Henrietta Seiberling, and she did belong
to the Wall Street magnate's family. She was his
daughter-in-law.

"And what can I do for you?" she asked.

Her voice was so charming and simple that Bill W.
answered without embarrassment.

"Well, you see, I'm an alcoholic, and I want to find
another alcoholic who needs help, so as to keep sober
myself. Could you put me in touch with one?"

Henrietta Seiberling didn't answer right away, and

Bill thought he had lost his last chance. Then, after a moment, the soft southern voice began again.

"I'm not an alcoholic," said Henrietta Seiberling; "all the same I've had some difficult moments along that line. And I think I understand. I do know a man you might help. Come to my house right away."

Henrietta Seiberling was not only charming and intelligent, but she seemed to have been especially chosen by fate to help Bill: she, too, had worked with the Oxford Group.

"The man I've got in mind is just the person you want," said the young woman. "His name is Bob S., but we all call him 'Dr. Bob.' He has a wonderful wife, Anne, and they have a son and a little adopted daughter. Bob is one of the best surgeons in town, but he drinks terribly. I know he wants to stop. Desperately. He's tried everything: medical cures and spiritual ones, including the Oxford Group's methods. He put his whole heart and will into it, but nothing did him any good. I'll call him up and ask him to come by with his wife."

It was Anne S. who answered the telephone. She apologized for not being able to come. But this Saturday was their anniversary, and Bob insisted on having a family celebration. He had even brought home a large evergreen plant.

Anne S. didn't add that the evergreen plant was standing on the table but her husband was lying under it, dead drunk, at that very moment—as Bill discovered later.

It was arranged that they should all meet for dinner next day at Henrietta Seiberling's. Dr. Bob and Anne arrived much earlier than they were expected, at about five o'clock in the afternoon. The surgeon kept having fits of spasmodic trembling, and muttered that he could only stop for a quarter of an hour.

Dr. Bob was a tall, heavily built man of about fifty-five, whereas Bill was not yet forty.

"He must be made of iron not to have been dead long ago," Bill said to himself. Then, since he knew by experience the only expedient to deal with the surgeon's terrible distress, the agonizing craving tormenting him, he advised him to take a large glass of liquor. Bob accepted it with some embarrassment, and felt prepared to face dinner—though, in fact, he couldn't touch a single dish.

Afterwards Henrietta Seiberling tactfully led the two men into a small library. They were there more than an hour.

Bill didn't conduct this conversation along the lines he had used with hundreds of alcoholics, always in vain. He thought he had discovered the reason for his failure. Carried away by his own mystical experience and the rarified theories of the Oxford Group, he had wanted to impose that difficult and high-principled pattern at once and at all costs on the most miserable of human wrecks.

What an absurd, childish way to set about things! It was not at all surprising that he had failed every time. When he was at his lowest, would he have listened to a half-mad, deluded preacher?

Then Bill remembered his own worst moments. The great light had only appeared when—and also because—he was emptied of all strength and pride, quite without hope, utterly defeated and out for the count, as it were.

"And what am I," thought Bill, "except an alcoholic among many others? What I must do is to reduce other people like me to the same state of utter despair I was in. But without subjecting them to moral pressure. They must reach this desperate state by their own volition. And that is only possible if they hear someone else who is equally seriously affected talking about himself. By my own example I must make them feel and experience that absolute void, and that will leave space for the necessary courage and determination to develop."

As a result of this train of reasoning—it was to become the golden rule for Alcoholics Anonymous—Bill didn't mention his own metaphysical experience during this first conversation with Dr. Bob. But he did give him an account of the damage drink had done to his own life, down to the most trivial detail.

The Akron surgeon listened with passionate interest to the Wall Street man's story. From time to time he would murmur, or even exclaim aloud without knowing it:

"Yes, it's just like that. . . ."

"Yes. Yes. It's the same with me. . . ."

Suddenly he began to talk himself, as he had never talked before. He laid bare his whole life, as it had been conditioned by drink.

.   .   .

◇◇◇

Like Bill W., Bob S. came from Vermont and belonged to an old Yankee family. His father had been a judge in that state, and was both feared and respected.

Bob started drinking very early, and was expelled from Dartmouth College for drunkenness, in spite of which he managed to finish his medical studies and his internship in Chicago. His failing didn't prevent him from showing exceptional skill as a surgeon.

After marrying Anne, he settled in the town of Akron and started a family there. But this didn't make him decide to give up drink; on the contrary, he indulged in it more and more. When his hands trembled so that he couldn't operate or examine a patient, he used to take strong doses of sedatives. And when even this device failed, he would disappear for a week into a clinic for disintoxication.

Even during these rare periods of sobriety, the frantic craving for drink never left him for an instant, and he always gave way to it as soon as he was free again.

When Dr. Bob met Bill W., thirty years of incessant alcoholism had left their mark on him.

Everything was crumbling around him. He had lost his job at the state hospital in Akron. Although his brilliance as a surgeon was universally recognized, very few of his colleagues or their patients dared trust him. His financial situation was so bad that he was threatened with dispossession and imprisonment. His wife was on the verge of a nervous breakdown. His children lived in terror. The whole family had forgotten what the word "hope" meant.

After the two men had exchanged their life histories, they found themselves suddenly drawn together by a feeling of organic sympathy and mutual confidence such as they had never before experienced. They were sick men suffering from the same disease, companions in trouble, accomplices in the same crime.

Then Bill W. spoke his mind freely. He didn't try to expound his spiritual theory to Dr. Bob, who was, as it happened, better informed on it than he was. Bill attacked his new friend physically, as it were.

He modified Dr. Silkworth's verdict on himself of "death or madness" to fit the surgeon's case. He demonstrated the inevitable rapid destruction of body and mind that would be his. He took the doctor down to the bottom of the pit, medically speaking.

Dr. Bob was appalled. Bill was better qualified than any psychiatrist or specialist: he was an alcoholic and knew what he was talking about.

And Bill, for his part, felt more convinced than ever before that in coping with Dr. Bob he was striking at alcoholism's grip on himself.

"I need him just as much as he needs me," he thought.

This idea, still vague and formless, contained within it the future development of Alcoholics Anonymous.

Next day, just as Bill W. was getting ready to go back

to New York, he unexpectedly received instructions
(and money from Wall Street) to continue the Akron
negotiations. When Dr. Bob's wife heard of this, she
begged Bill W. to come and stay with them.

After three weeks of complete sobriety, during
which the two alcoholics talked and planned together
every day, Dr. Bob said to his friend in his wife's presence:

"Bill, I've been going to our annual medical congress
in Atlantic City for a long time. It's quite soon now.
Don't you think I ought to go?"

"Oh no! no!" cried Anne in dismay.

She knew American habits. Medical congresses were
just like political ones, or like meetings of the American
Legion, or of engineers or commercial travelers, or of
any other body. Such reunions of men who had escaped
from domestic worries and their wives' watchful eyes
always ended in terrific drinking.

But Bill didn't agree. He said to Dr. Bob:

"Why not go? After all, we've got to learn to live in
an alcohol-soaked society."

"I rather think you may be right," said Dr. Bob slowly.

He went, and for several days there was no news of
him. One morning the nurse from his office telephoned.

"He's at my house," she said. "My husband and I
picked him up off the station platform at four o'clock
this morning, dead drunk."

Anne and Bill brought Dr. Bob home and carried
him to bed unconscious. Anne was in despair, for she
remembered that her husband was due to perform a

difficult surgical operation. What was particularly serious was that he was the only man capable of carrying it out and that the patient's condition made it impossible to postpone it more than another three days.

Three more days at the very most, and Bill had already spent a desperate week of delirium, shivering convulsively till his teeth chattered.

Anne and Bill took turns watching over the alcoholic. Bill spent the night before the decisive morning in Dr. Bob's room and dozed off for a few hours. When he awoke, he saw his friend's eyes fixed on his face with an expression he would never forget. Dr. Bob had regained full consciousness and all his faculties, but he was still shaking uncontrollably.

"Look, Bill," said the surgeon, "I'm determined to make it."

Bill thought he meant the operation.

"No," said Dr. Bob. "I'm talking of the problem we've so often discussed together."

At nine o'clock, Anne and Bill took Dr. Bob to the clinic. Once there, Bill gave him a bottle of beer to steady his hand. The surgeon went into the operating room, and Anne and Bill went home.

They waited for what seemed an interminable time. At last the telephone rang. Everything had gone off all right. But in spite of the terrible nervous strain Dr. Bob had been subjected to, he didn't come home at once. He first went to see everyone he owed money to, or had done any injury to, to set things straight.

This was on June 10, 1935. From that day until his

death fifteen years later, Dr. Bob never once touched liquor. He got back his health, his skill, his material prosperity, and his happiness at home.

And, even more important, Alcoholics Anonymous was born.

Early next morning Dr. Bob said to Bill W.:

"Don't you think it's desperately important that we should get to work on other alcoholics? And that that's the way to ensure our own safety?"

"That's exactly what we must do," Bill said. "But where to find them?"

"There's never any shortage at the municipal hospital," Dr. Bob assured him.

They went there. A nurse whom Dr. Bob had known a long time, and whose job it was to receive patients, pointed out the most difficult case she had: a man who had just been brought in in the middle of an attack of delirium tremens. He had hit several nurses in the face and had been put to bed in a straight jacket.

Dr. Bob prescribed medication, had the firmly secured alcoholic moved to a private room, and gave orders to be informed as soon as he came to his senses.

Two days later the two friends arrived at the patient's bedside. He was lucid now but in a state of frightful depression. Bill and Dr. Bob took turns describing their own experiences and offering him their moral support.

"Thanks, boys," said the old man, shaking his head despairingly. "You've managed to snap out of it, and that's wonderful. But there's nothing to be done for me.

I'm such a bad case that I'm afraid to leave the hospital and find myself alone outside. And don't talk to me about religion, either. I was deacon of my church for a while. And I still believe in God. But I'm not at all sure He believes in me."

"All right," said Dr. Bob. "Maybe you'll feel better tomorrow. Would you like to see us again?"

"Certainly," said the sick man. "Not that it'll make any difference. But I'd be very glad to see you both. At least you know what you're talking about."

When Bill and Dr. Bob went to see the old alcoholic next day, his wife was with him, and he said to her:

"Here are the two boys who understand me."

Then he told his visitors what sort of a night he'd had. He had stayed awake till dawn, feeling more and more depressed. When it was worst and he felt he could bear it no more, he thought to himself: "If those two could make it, so can I." He had repeated this over and over, and suddenly he felt sure of himself. And with that he fell asleep.

And this same man who the evening before had been trembling at the idea of leaving the hospital was now telling his wife to go and get his clothes, that he was going home at once. He, too, succeeded in keeping off alcohol for the rest of his life.

He was the third member of Alcoholics Anonymous. Dr. Bob and he made up the first group, the Akron group.

From now on things began to move. And they have not stopped since.

◇◇◇

At first it was slow and difficult. In 1939, that is to say after four years, the founders of A. A. had only acquired a hundred followers. And what financial, administrative, and moral vicissitudes they suffered! And how terrible it was to witness a relapse, perhaps among those who had seemed most steadfast and enthusiastic. Ebby, for instance, who was responsible for Bill W.'s seeing the light, succumbed to alcohol once more, finally and fatally.

When Bill and Lois W. began taking alcoholics into their Brooklyn house, they had to deal with brawls and a suicide.

But nothing could stop the movement from spreading. It had taken shape; its methods and the results achieved (although they were not yet numerous) astonished everyone who heard about them.

In 1941 *The Saturday Evening Post* published an article about Alcoholics Anonymous. There were discussions on the radio and in the newspapers. The avalanche had been set in motion. Today there are more than 300,000 members in the United States; and more than eighty countries in the world, some of them tiny and remote, have their own groups. Doctors, psychiatrists, lawyers, priests, and prison governors all consult A. A.

That is what I was told, in that bare little room in Alcoholics Anonymous' general offices, by Bill W., co-founder of the association with Dr. Bob. He had devoted himself wholly to it for a quarter of a century.

Before I left I asked:

"What about the material aspect? Do you draw a salary?"

"No," Bill told me.

"What, then?" I persisted.

"Well," Bill said, "at first my wife went on working in the store. Afterwards I wrote two books, which I see you have, about our beginnings, our growth, and our problems. They sell well enough to bring in a living."

He began to laugh, adding:

"A modest one, of course. But I left all my dreams of luxury and splendor in Wall Street long ago."

I walked through the premises of A. A. in a sort of trance.

When I reached the passage leading to the elevator, I was confronted by reality again. It took the form of a fantastically thin, hairy little man dressed in rags, with chattering teeth in spite of the warmth of the building. His every pore exuded an appalling stench of sour alcohol and dirt.

I instinctively offered him money. He put out his hand, drew it back, and put it out again, stammering:

"I oughtn't to . . . no . . . I oughtn't to."

He took it all the same, and stared at me with glazed, bleary, bloodshot eyes. And, speaking with difficulty through his chattering teeth, he said:

"Been wanting to come in for the last hour and haven't had the courage."

He leaned against the wall, closed his eyes, and seemed to fall asleep.

I left him there. But I remember thinking:

"If he does go into the A. A. offices, or if he screws up his courage some other day, perhaps that piece of human refuse might turn into another Bill W."

For I now knew that anything was possible.

PART TWO

VIII

Admission Free

During the last twenty-five years, dozens and dozens of thousands of supposedly incurable drunks have been restored to sobriety—and therefore to health, work, dignity, and a normal life—by Alcoholics Anonymous.

There is nothing mysterious about the method that has succeeded where all others have failed. It's very simple to describe. But in order to understand it properly, we must keep two unfamiliar factors in mind: the special form alcoholism takes in the United States and the new theory of the disease put forward by the extraordinary association that has sprung out of it.

It's well known that most Americans who take to drink are attracted more by the effect than by the taste. It's not necessary to cross the Atlantic to discover this fact. Plenty of tourists have demonstrated it in Europe.

Should one look for the explanation in the absence of

◇◇

a tradition of vinegrowing? Or in the violent extremes
of climate? the vastness of the open spaces so stubbornly and recently conquered, and the feeling of
solitude they inspire? the sexual prudery of the
Puritans? unbearable boredom?

Whatever the physical and moral reasons may be,
they are less important than the fact itself: that the
American who drinks heavily does so as an escape. He
longs to be bludgeoned into unconsciousness.

I was aware of this. But I was astounded to discover
that for thousands of men and women (gradually or
rapidly, according to temperament) alcohol ceases to be
a means and becomes an end in itself. They don't drink
to be able to stay alive; they drink for the sake of drinking—and in the end so as to feel nothing any more and
plunge into oblivion.

How many members of Alcoholics Anonymous have
I not listened to—either at public meetings or in private
conversation—telling of those interminable tête à
têtes with a bottle, which is emptied and refilled again
and again until the drinker is paralyzed both physically
and mentally. They described their total lack of interest
in families, jobs, material security, self-respect, or
elementary hygiene. And their fatal, almost mathemati-
cal decline. How their resources dwindled. They would
drink stuff of viler and viler quality. The sordid stinking
room, the best they could afford. After that the street.
And the perpetual fear of going short of liquor. And
the months spent in prisons, clinics for disintoxication,
mental homes.

◇◇

Exactly like the most confirmed drug addicts.

That isn't the whole story. The same people would describe in detail, as if it were an ordinary event in their lives, what they called "blackouts," complete losses of lucidity.

Any man who has at times drunk to excess knows what it is to wake uneasy because he can't remember what he did the night before. But what a difference between these brief gaps in memory and the days and weeks of total loss and emptiness familiar to alcoholics. And what about those crazy adventures, journeys of three thousand miles from one end of the continent to the other, which leave behind no recollection of how, why, or where the persons went, only that they were drinking all the time?

They are lucky that they don't find themselves behind bars when they come to their senses.

The phrase "go on a binge" comes to mind to describe these extravagant peregrinations. But though it's easy to imagine a sailor needing to break out when he reaches land after his long confinement on board ship, or the inhabitants of the flophouses being fascinated by the warmth and light of the Bowery bars, it is astonishing to find this compulsion toward sudden, total, disastrous flight from reality on the part of people who seem to have everything that makes life worth living: health, money, and fame.

Nevertheless, in the United States men and women favored by the two gods Americans adore—money and success—make up the largest proportion of far-gone

◇◇

alcoholics. In the world of business, politics, literature, journalism, medicine, the theater, the movies, and television, there are many of both sexes who have been engulfed by alcoholism or are struggling desperately on the brink. The names of these people, and the brilliance of their past combined with the suddenness of their fall, make the brain reel.

It would seem that their free, rich life is less tolerable to them than flophouses are to the poor or confinement to the sailor. It suffocates them. They fall prey to anxiety and fear; and to escape from these torments, they jump into the abyss itself.

However incredible we may find this mad rush toward self-destruction, this slow suicide on the part of fortune's favorites, it did not surprise the two founders of Alcoholics Anonymous. They belonged to this privileged class: before drink had ruined their lives, Bill W. had done extremely well on Wall Street and Dr. Bob had been a brilliant surgeon.

They knew that the motive for this disastrous disease could be neither poverty nor failure. And it could not be looked for at home: they were both married to wonderful women, who had stood by them and supported them through the worst financial, physical, and psychological crises.

They realized that if under such conditions they had taken to drink so desperately as to lose their senses and all desire for life, it was because alcoholism was pathologically necessary to them, an obsession.

However, that was not a sufficient explanation.

How was it that other men, young or old, friends they had made in their schooldays, the army, or at work, at parties or in bars, could make a habit of drinking often and heavily and still keep within the limits of a regular, secure life? How was it that even drinking to excess did not for them set going that terrible chain reaction that darkened and destroyed everything? How was it that they were still in command of themselves and their lives even when they were drinking? In fact, how did some people control their drinking, whereas others— like Bill and Dr. Bob—became slaves to it?

What essential quality did the latter lack?

Education? No. Bill W. and Dr. Bob had had the best that was available in one of the most cultured and civilized regions of the United States; and they had been brought up in the bosom of families with a tradition of dignity and decent behavior. Yet they both knew plenty of less polished men who hadn't been dragged down by drink.

Religion? Not that, either. Both had been pious as children, and spiritual questions had interested them all their lives. Yet many agnostics, atheists, and materialists could enjoy drink without letting it get the upper hand.

Will power? That wasn't the answer, either. Bill W. and Dr. Bob had both known that they had more than most of their acquaintances, so far as everything except the battle against intoxication was concerned.

Personal relationships? They both adored their wives,

were tried friends, and aroused sympathy and affection wherever they went. In spite of all this, they brought ruin and despair on those who loved them and whom they loved most, whereas confirmed egotists often provided a decent, secure, and peaceful life for their families, just because they knew when to stop drinking.

Thinking over all the available data, Bill W. and Dr. Bob arrived at a strange new theory of alcoholism which was of fundamental importance to themselves, and later to hundreds of thousands of men and women whom they persuaded to share it.

Since some people apparently blessed with everything that should save them from alcoholism—a loving home in childhood, money, success, happy marriage, friends—take to drink uncontrollably, whereas others much less well-endowed by fate can drink without crossing the fatal frontier, a certain conclusion is inevitable:

One does not *become an alcoholic*. One is *born* an alcoholic.

But the congenital nature of the disease does not imply that the vice itself is inherited—for many drunks come of abstemious parents; or that it is a major defect of mind or body—because many alcoholics start drinking when they are in the best of health physically and mentally. In short, after studying and analyzing their own cases and many similar ones intimately known to them, Bill W. and Dr. Bob came to the conclusion that alcoholism was a predisposition belonging

◇◇◇

to the often inexplicable and little understood domain of *allergy*, or organic intolerance.

There are people who are seriously affected by certain foods or medicines (even in infinitesimal quantities), or by contact with some normally harmless plants, or by certain smells. A tiny piece of egg or a drop of quinine may act like poison on them.

It is impossible to detect such abnormal sensibility in advance, or to discover the chemical cause of this toxic reaction. Experience is the only guide.

It is the same with intolerance, or allergy, to alcohol.

It divides the human race into two categories.

Those in the first category are, of course, liable to be affected in heart, kidneys, liver, and nerves by excessive drinking (more or less, according to their powers of resistance), but it will not attack their very existence, warping and destroying it. It is merely a harmful element in their lives, like oversmoking or overeating.

But for those in the other category—the allergics— alcohol is not just a contributory cause of illness; it is an illness in itself, and a fatal one. The predisposition they were born with means that each glass gives them an irresistible longing for another, and then for a third, and so on, until they are insensible. It means that even when they come to their senses and realize their danger, their obsession with drink is still too strong for their will power. It means that drink becomes their sole purpose in life and drags them down inevitably into bestial sottishness, ruin, prison, or the lunatic asylum, according to circumstances.

Bill W. often uses the following analogy to bring home his definition of alcoholism:

"We all know," he says, "that sugar is harmless or even beneficial to most people, but there are some to whom it is dangerous or even deadly. I mean those born with a predisposition to diabetes. They only discover their disease by the harmful effects sugar produces on their organisms. Then their allergy is recognized, and they are put on a special diet.

"All this is true also of alcoholics: congenital predisposition, allergy, and necessary discipline. In their case the harmful agency is not sugar but drink. That is the sole difference."

I'm not qualified to judge this definition of alcoholism as a potential disease (like an open wound) existing in certain organisms and causing alcohol to act on them like some destructive microbe. But it is an accepted law among members of Alcoholics Anonymous, and they after all have a deeper understanding of the disease, a wider field of observation, and more reason to think about it than anyone else. In addition, the number of eminent doctors and psychiatrists in the United States who believe this theory to be the one closest to the truth is growing every day.

In any case, if we are to explore the source of the astonishing work Alcoholics Anonymous have done, we must not for a moment forget their theory of alcoholism; we must accustom ourselves to its effect both on their way of thought and on their vocabulary.

It isn't always easy: especially when they seem to

have changed the meaning of some of our deepest-rooted notions and ways of expressing ourselves on the subject.

A typical example in my own case was a dinner given in a large restaurant by some of the most famous members of Alcoholics Anonymous for friends who didn't belong to the association. All the guests took very strong cocktails before they sat down to eat; some took three or four. During dinner they drank beer or wine. Afterwards, some asked for brandy. Meanwhile, our hosts were drinking water, iced tea, lemonade, or coffee, according to taste. None of them had touched alcohol in any form for ten months at least, and there were some who had abstained much longer.

Yet I soon noticed that the man at my right, a white-haired banker and a veteran member of Alcoholics Anonymous, always said "we alcoholics" when referring to himself or his absolutely sober fellow members, but never when he was talking of his steadily drinking guests.

"But, good heavens," I said to him, "even if you were once alcoholics, all that was years and years ago, whereas. . . ."

My neighbor interrupted me gently:

"My friend, you know our basic definition: one does not become an alcoholic, one is born an alcoholic. It follows from that that one never stops being one. Abstinence is just as necessary to us as it is effective. But it isn't a final cure. There is none against our allergy."

◇◇

"Then you mean that any man or woman I see here who hasn't touched a drop since 1940. . . ."

"Is still an alcoholic," said the white-haired banker. "And would be even if he had abstained since 1920."

Seeing my incredulous expression, he produced Alcoholics Anonymous' favorite analogy.

"Take a diabetic," he said. "Thanks to his diet and medical treatment, he can lead an active, normal life. But he is never *cured*. He still has diabetes and is condemned to a strict discipline. It's just the same with us."

The old banker laughed, and went on:

"Do you know how we differentiate between sober alcoholics and those who are not? We call the latter drinking drunks and the others *nondrinking drunks*."

A fat red-faced man sitting opposite us refilled his glass with strong beer, and swallowed it with obvious relish. My neighbor watched him, and I couldn't tell whether his expression was one of envy, regret, admiration, or relief.

"You see," he said to me, "there you have the whole thing: our friend opposite came into the world with a constitution that tolerates alcohol. He drinks every day without any effect on his life. I'm in a very good position to know. We have common interests in some important businesses and are fellow members of a good many boards of directors."

This "alcoholic" whose palate for the last twenty

years had not known the taste of alcohol smiled pensively as he looked at the "nonalcoholic" who had taken a daily ration of several cocktails ever since adolescence.

"In our view, being an alcoholic is not a question of the quantity taken but of the way the organism tolerates it," my neighbor went on. "If you can drink two bottles of whisky a day and still be in full control of your life, you aren't an alcoholic. Example: Winston Churchill. If your allergy makes you forget everything else in the world after a single glass and drags you, by a series of drinking bouts, lower and lower—why, then you are an alcoholic. And will be until you die. Example: me."

I was silent for a few minutes, trying to adapt my mind to these new ideas, so different from those I had held on the subject up to now. Then I said to the old banker:

"But surely there are a great many subtle degrees between these two extremes?"

"Sure," said my neighbor.

"Well, when it comes to the borderline, how do you recognize an alcoholic?"

"Only someone personally involved can do so," said the old man.[1] "And that is another of our basic principles."

Cigars and liqueurs were handed around. I took a Havana cigar and a glass of brandy and tried to

[1] See Appendix for the questionnaire suggested by A. A. to help determine the difference.

memorize the principles of the method that several weeks with Alcoholics Anonymous had taught me.

Today the doctrines of Alcoholics Anonymous are precise, clear, and complete; and an adaptable and coherent system has been framed for putting them into practice. But it took a quarter of a century of trial and experiment to reach this position. Step by step, carefully feeling their way, correcting mistakes, adapting working hypotheses to human material and the mysterious behavior of the disease, A. A. have developed a definite and effective procedure from the preliminary theory.

It had all begun with Bill W. Ruined by drink and brought back to sobriety from the very gates of madness and death by religious revelation, he was (after only six months as an abstainer) suddenly seized in a strange town by the urge to rescue another alcoholic from disaster in order to save himself. It was a sort of miracle that he should at the very last minute have found the man he wanted in Dr. Bob, who had reached the brink of final catastrophe through drunkenness.

By joining forces to fight against their common trouble, these two men laid the foundations of Alcoholics Anonymous without knowing it, and formulated their first golden rule: an alcoholic will listen to another alcoholic with more confidence than to anyone else, and the man who has come to his help is helping himself as well.

Everything started from that. Bill W. and Dr. Bob

undertook their task with boundless enthusiasm and devotion, because they were as deeply committed to it by their own need for safety as by their desire to help others. Every day their own sobriety was strengthened by their efforts to rescue other poor devils. For the daily sight of a degradation they had so narrowly escaped themselves increased their terror of a relapse; and by impressing reasons for hope on others, they renewed their own belief.

It turned out that this first conclusion of theirs, based solely on the experience of two people, could be generally applied. Men who had become abject wrecks, and for whom doctors, lawyers, teachers, and priests could do nothing, suddenly dragged themselves out of their sodden degradation, their impotence and despair, when they heard what Bill W. or Dr. Bob had to say, and forced themselves to begin the struggle all over again. And they triumphed in the end.

Why? Because they weren't confronted by people who wanted to reform them in the name of religion, science, or law; people who made them feel ashamed, afraid, or inferior; people with the best intentions but who were all the same strangers, unaffected by their disease and unable to understand it.

With Bill or Dr. Bob everything was different. From their first words the alcoholics recognized that here were men like themselves. Trembling fits, ghastly awakenings, dreadful anxiety; the low, ignominious tricks they had stooped to in order to get another bottle, or another glass—these two men couldn't possibly have described them so faithfully had they not known at first hand what they were talking about. They had suffered all these horrors. They had been themselves, without doubt or question, in the grip of alcoholism.

Then their hearers would gradually lose their tormenting embarrassment or morbid pride, forget about their dirt, rags, and foul breath—even their hidden but terrible sense of guilt. The arguments would find no barrier, but penetrate minds ready to receive them, for they were childishly simple and obvious.

"You see," Bill or Bob would say, "you're not a leper or a criminal; you're simply a sick man, a man with an allergy. You can be cured. We've had the same disease, and sunk much lower than you and been closer to madness and death. Yet here we are, sober, safe. You've only got to do the same. And you can. We'll help you."

The unfortunate wretch would look at these men who had suffered from the same disease, behaved as shamefully, and been damned in the same hell, and see that they were clean, well dressed, and full of energy, the joy of life, and brotherly feeling.

And since man hardly ever accepts his own utter decline and destruction without some revolt of the instincts, the living corpse would find himself thinking: "Why not me, too?" Then he would try to get hold of himself, this time putting an energy and enthusiasm into his efforts that he had never had before, because this time he really believed—he saw safety written on the faces of these new companions in trouble.

Some were successful at the first attempt, and others

only after one or more relapses. There were many who could never defeat the monster. But those who got away had only one desire: to announce their new discovery to other alcoholics and show them the way. They knew also that in trying to revive others they were protecting that fragile plant—their own return to life.

Even without that special reason it is easy to understand their desire to convert others. We have only to think of people who have at last been cured of a very long and serious illness. How insistently and zealously they recommend their cure, doctor, medicines, or spas to others who suffer from the same disease! They feel an urgent need to share their own good fortune.

In the reformed alcoholic this very natural desire has unusual strength. For his disease—apart from the physical troubles it brings in its wake—is a disease of solitude, anxiety, and despair. When he is once free of all this, it seems like a miracle, and he feels the need to proclaim the fact. Only the miserable wretches who could be saved by that miracle can measure its amazing virtue. Everyone who experiences it feels in turn the same urgent desire to spread the light. Thus the chain is formed and goes on indefinitely adding new links.

Today there is at least one group of Alcoholics Anonymous in even the remotest and most isolated regions of the United States; and basic literature, leaflets, and an intelligent and lively monthly review are available to all; doctors, priests, novelists, and scriptwriters have taken the association and its members as their theme;

columns are given over to it in the newspapers; whole programs, on radio and television. In short, everything has been done to draw the attention of alcoholics to their disease, convince them that they can be cured, and indicate first-aid stations and the means of summoning help.

But in the early pioneering days—as the veterans of Alcoholics Anonymous call them—the only instrument of propaganda was personal conversation, from sick man to sick man, from one alcoholic to another.

What a remarkable mission of mercy! A man only just out of the gutter or the hospital, still marked by the ravages of the drink he had given up, would return to the hospital or the gutter in order to save someone like himself and ensure his own safety by so doing.

The earliest reformed alcoholics who followed Bill W. and Dr. Bob thought of nothing else but this recruiting campaign. But when it began to bear fruit and new groups of A. A. saw the light in one town after another, it became necessary to solve a fundamental problem: under what conditions ought Alcoholics Anonymous to accept a new member? As always happens everywhere, there were two opposing camps: one in favor of severity, and another, of tolerance.

The first said:

"We have room only for decent alcoholics, confirmed abstainers. We mustn't hesitate to exclude anyone who relapses, and we must refuse admittance to people who arrive at our meetings drunk."

✧✧✧

To which the others replied:

"Our association isn't a club. The words 'admit' and 'exclude' are incompatible with our vacabulary, our function, and our principles. 'Alcoholics speaking to other alcoholics'—that is the only justification for our existence. It's ludicrous to pretend that one alcoholic can judge another. Which of us has the right to discriminate, to throw the first stone?

"There are no deserving and undeserving alcoholics; there are only people who are more or less seriously ill. Remember our first conclusion, the first truth we discovered: in helping others you are above all helping yourself. The harder the task, the more good it does to the man who undertakes it. The greater difficulty a pupil has in regaining his sobriety, the more certain his friends and tutors can be of preserving their own."

"In any case," said the partisans of strictness, "one can't help discriminating between honest and dishonest people, normal people and perverts. We cannot accept anyone whose sexual life is against nature, or anyone who shows contempt for the law."

"Absolutely wrong," replied their more broadminded adversaries. "Alcoholics Anonymous is not a moral institution nor a school for citizenship. Alcoholics must stick together—very little else matters. As for prostitutes, homosexuals, drug addicts, thieves, murderers even—how is their disease different from ours?"

"But, then, in that case," cried the puritans, "what rules can we have? Where are we to draw the line?"

"There must be none; any alcoholic who crosses our threshold is welcome, whatever he is like," said the humanists.

They were in the majority. They carried the day, and experience shows that they were right.

It is impossible to conceive of a less exacting, freer, more open association than Alcoholics Anonymous. A new member has no forms to fill out, no subscription to pay, no pledge of any sort to make. He only has to walk in and say: "I am an alcoholic. I want to try to stop drinking."

The miracle—or rather one among many—is that this vague, anarchic system has succeeded so well. Collective conscience, patience, and joint responsibility have won a victory over some of the most rebellious cases.

"Every A. A. 'old timer' shudders with remorse today when he thinks of his own harshness in the past," Bill W. said to me one day. "The people we declared would never come back, or ought to be expelled for the good of the movement—well, plenty of them have been sober for years and have become some of our best members. Where would they be now if everyone in their group had judged them so severely?"

The founder of Alcoholics Anonymous gently shook his white head. His eyes lit up his lean face with a characteristic twinkle of mischief.

"I know one group," he said laughing, "where you'll find a senator, a lady famous for her lack of virtue, a Catholic priest, the president of five large banks, a judge, and one of Al Capone's thugs—all sitting side by side at the weekly meeting.

"You see, alcoholism is like the army: you meet everyone there. Though the army finds it more difficult than we do to get recruits."

Bill W.'s face became serious again, and he went on:

"It's perfectly natural that there should be a lot of habitual criminals in A. A. Alcohol is one of the determining causes of half the crimes and misdemeanors there are. Those who realize this come to us when they leave prison. That doesn't mean that they all reform, or anyhow not immediately. And we do get the crime squad and the F.B.I. appearing sometimes at our meetings."

His eyes sparkled with amusement again.

"It's only fair to say that there's a whole group of A. A. entirely composed of policemen," said Bill W.

"Then, a man or woman of any nationality, creed, color, religious and political opinion, or morals can join A. A. without obligation or undertaking of any kind?" I asked.

"We would take the Devil himself if he were an alcoholic and needed our help," said Bill W.

IX

The First Glass

All members of Alcoholics Anonymous—however they may differ in origin, wealth, intelligence, and education, whether they be white, black, or yellow, millionaires or paupers, devout believers or obstinate atheists, capitalists or Communists—must practice the same methods and follow the same road to sobriety.

The first stages of the procedure are almost childishly simple.

Each new arrival has a sponsor—that is, a godfather, tutor, and mentor who is an established member of A. A. The person (man or woman) who carries out this function does so either because he has persuaded an alcoholic friend to join the association or because an alcoholic has come to him of his own accord and chosen him out of instinctive trust and sympathy.

It is not an easy task. The sponsor—who is never paid for his work—has to look after someone tortured by cramps, attacks of anxiety, fits of rage, and insomnia as a result of abstaining from drink. And the remedy for all these torments is easily available at the corner of every street, behind the gaudy neon signs of bars or the more modest signs of liquor stores.

The sponsor struggles with his pupil against the frenzies and nostalgia he has known so well himself. The memory of his own suffering gives him the power to understand, and also the necessary compassion, courage, and persistence. His time is no longer his own. He neglects his profession and his family, for it is vital that he should be available whenever he is wanted. He must hurry to answer a summons even if it comes when he is hard at work or fast asleep. A few moments may make all the difference.

If he arrives in time, he can calm the panting, desperate, half-distracted wretch who has just shouted "Help!" from the telephone booth of some bar or street corner; he can deflect him from his obsessional idea. If the man's wife, brother, or child calls him, the case is even more urgent, for it means that the sufferer himself has lost his faith in everything and everyone except alcohol and will have recourse to it again if his sponsor arrives a minute too late. Then all his efforts will have been in vain. Everything will have to be done again, if indeed he is ready to have another try after his relapse.

For something worse than satisfying a deep physical craving has happened: he has rediscovered his old way of life and reason for living.

The sponsor, too, has been involved in this exhausting struggle and taken a few unsteady steps toward the empty horizon. He knows that it is as cruel and futile to say to an alcoholic on the verge of mental disintoxication: "You must never drink again," as to force a traveler to leave a country full of gushing springs for a limitless desert.

That is why he takes every opportunity of insinuating into a new member's mind the first practical precepts laid down by A. A.

The first basic rule that the tutor tries to instil into his pupil's mind has the advantage of being very simple.

"From now on," he says, "you must stop thinking more than a day ahead. Forget about all the rest of your life after that. Forget about weeks, months, and years. Don't swear any oaths or make any pledges; only imagine the efforts you're going to make during the next twenty-four hours. Concentrate all your energies, pray to whatever God you believe in, appeal to your love for your wife, fortify yourself (if everything else fails) by my example or that of the other members of A. A., so as to stay sober for the coming twenty-four hours only. Fix your mind on the ticking of the clock. Think only of holding out till the last minute of these twenty-four hours. Ask yourself no questions about 'afterwards.' Keep your mind shut and empty. And when you hear the hour you've been waiting for strike, begin over again willing with all your might and main—but only for another twenty-four hours."

◇◇◇

If the newcomer succeeds in carrying out this very simple mental exercise—and more often than not he does—he is on tho way to being saved. Because after counting every second of the first twenty-four hours, he thinks to himself: "I've got through today without drinking. Why not another day, just one more?" It has already become easier. So he advances towards sobriety along this strange, mental cog railway.

The sponsor's influence is not the only one the newcomer is subjected to. The sponsor, like all members of A. A., belongs to a group, and he gets his pupil to join it. There is an open meeting of each group every week, always preceded by a special session for new recruits, as well as closed meetings where individual problems are discussed and anyone may make a contribution.

In larger towns and cities these groups are numerous. In New York there are hundreds of them, and at least fifty meetings take place every day and at all hours. There are also restaurants, and clubs reserved for Alcoholics Anonymous and their friends. The newcomer is pressed to go to them as often as possible, especially to the group meetings.

As a rule, he has time on his hands. Too much time. He had to touch rock bottom before he decided to try to keep sober. His money is all gone; he has no job. His marriage has broken up. His friends are bored, irritated, and disgusted with him. He is quite alone, unoccupied, discouraged, confronting the bare, icy steppe of existence. What's to be done? Take to drink again? And beg, steal, or assault a passer-by to get it?

No. This man who doesn't know which way to turn can take refuge in the groups and establishments of A. A. In all of them, at any time of day or even late at night, he will find people *like himself.*

Some of them have been sober for many long years. Others only knocked off drink quite recently. The former show no signs of their old wounds. The scars of the latter are fresh and bleeding. Never mind: both will welcome him with complete friendliness and good-fellowship. They see themselves in him, just as he sees himself in them. A warm brotherly sympathy unites these gatherings of survivors.

The new arrival hears everyone around him talking of problems that also concern him deeply. He can go into his own at length. He'll be listened to with gratifying attention. He's one of the family. And since there's no absolute standard of human suffering, however terrible his own experiences have been he's sure to find someone else who has been through worse. He begins to hope. He thinks to himself: "If even this poor wretch got free, then all the more chance for me."

Eagerly and with fresh confidence he listens to the advice of his friends around him, and the rules and laws of health and safety gradually sink into his mind.

Among these articles of faith, he is constantly warned that the first glass is of prime importance.

The reformed alcoholic who is still tormented by his craving for drink has to fight against one final false hope, the biggest illusion of all. It consists of thinking

◇◇◇

—or rather of wanting to think: "One glass can't do me any harm. Only one."

The answer given by Alcoholics Anonymous is this:

"There is no such thing as 'only one glass' for us congenital allergics. That glass is only the first, and by the nature of our disease it will set going an uncontrollable, disastrous chain reaction. That first glass will become two, three, and ten; then one, two, three, and ten bottles. And you'll be back where you started: in the gutter, in despair.

"And don't say: 'I know to my cost what the danger is. Only one glass, that's all.' By saying that, you're believing what you want to believe, making excuses for your obsessional craving. You won't stop. You can't. Other people who have kept sober longer than you and more stubbornly have been taken in by that illusion. It never is the 'only glass'; it's the 'first glass.' And that glass—the 'only one,' as you say—has dragged them down to the most abject wretchedness again."

Every sponsor hammers home this truth for the benefit of the newcomer in his charge. It comes up at every meeting for new recruits. It is confirmed by the life stories related at the open meetings. And what stories they are!

Lives are rebuilt after a painful struggle; material security returns, peace of mind and happiness begin to flower again—and then comes the *first glass*. And complete, blind relapse. And hell once more.

I have heard many terrifying stories bearing on this

topic, stories that made me feel physically ill. But when I showed the horror mixed with incredulity which I felt, I was told:

"Well, go and see N. He really was an extreme case."

I followed this advice with alacrity. I had a particular reason for being interested, quite apart from my research. N. is, as it happens, an exceptionally talented writer, and I would have been glad to meet him under any circumstances. After the war, he published an admirable novel with an alcoholic for the hero, and the book had a great success all over the world.

N. invited me to lunch with him at Ansa. This is one of the clubs run by Alcoholics Anonymous, and is housed on the ground floor of the Columbia University Club building. It is reached through an ancient, thickly carpeted, paneled passage hung with venerable portraits of the more eminent professors and the more generous benefactors.

But the club itself was not in the least academic. It was decorated in gay fresh colors and simply furnished, and everyone there seemed friendly and cheerful.

I recognized several whom I had met before at group meetings or else privately: a banker, an actor, a young woman who had tried to commit suicide three times before joining the association; and Kay, the old lady who had for a long time had a paralyzed tongue and vocal chords after drink had dragged her into the gutter.

A small bald red-faced man about fifty years old detached himself from this lively, noisy, friendly crowd so like any New York club crowd. He had a clipped

◇◇◇

mustache and wore glasses. His high forehead shone like polished copper. His fine, rather narrow, reddish-brown eyes shone humorously from behind his glasses. It was N.

When we had ordered our lunch, I begged him to tell me the story of his life, with many apologies for my professional inquisitiveness.

"Apologies for what?" he exclaimed. "Quite unnecessary. I'm delighted. You don't seem to realize that we alcoholics are the greatest barefaced show-offs in the world."

His eyes were so full of mischief, intelligence, and good humor that the thick lenses of his glasses seemed to sparkle.

"I began writing when I was sixteen," said N. "But I didn't want to publish anything till I was forty. Meanwhile I earned my living writing bombastic or sentimental stories for the radio. Nonsense, in fact. At the same time I was drinking appallingly. I had become a professional alcoholic; and I was heading for disaster. I realized what was happening. And I stopped drinking altogether, entirely on my own."

A large jovial man stopped at our table on his way out of the dining room.

"Hello, Jack," he said. "Will we see you tomorrow?"

"No," said N. "I'm going to Texas tomorrow. I've got to address some of our groups there."

The man went out, and N. took up his story.

"Yes," he said, "I stopped entirely without help, and by my own will power. You can imagine what sort of a reception I gave people who came and sang the praises of Alcoholics to me. What had I in common with these simple souls, with their mystical blah-blah, these weaklings who had to huddle together so as to meet the shock? I was an intellectual, a superior being."

"Then, at the time your novel came out," I asked, "you weren't drinking?"

"I hadn't tasted alcohol in any shape or form for eight years," said the novelist.

For the first time I noticed a melancholy expression come into his reddish-brown, oriental eyes.

"And I had a success," he went on, "such as I shall never have again. First the book, then the film; ecstatic reviews, enormous sums in royalties. I bought a fine house in New York and another in the country. I sent my two daughters to the most expensive private schools. And in spite of my success, which really might have turned the coolest head, I still kept off drink."

N.'s eyes were twinkling again.

"However," he said, "A. A.'s reputation was spreading all the time. I laughed at it, and yet I was exasperated by it. What could these chattering, gregarious people tell me—the man who had written a classic on alcoholism, publicly referred to by doctors and psychiatrists specializing in the subject? The man, too, who had kept sober for eleven years without the slightest relapse?"

N. cheerfully rubbed his shining copper-colored forehead and went on:

"Thereupon, rich, proud, and very pleased with my-

self, I went off to Bermuda for a holiday. It's a paradise.
But there are times when it's very hot there. And, one
day, simply on account of the heat, I longed for some
ice-cold beer. It's madness, I thought immediately; I've
not touched alcohol for eleven years. I'm not going to
start now. And the intellectual part of me replied: 'Exactly; after eleven years of complete abstinence a glass
of beer can't possibly do you any harm.' Hell! Only one
glass! After eleven years! Just one glass!

N. went on rubbing his polished forehead and smiling.

"And then?" I asked.

"Then," said the novelist, "the result of this 'one glass'
of beer was that in the next eighteen months I was
taken *fifteen times* to mental homes in a desperate
state of alcoholism. Yes, me, the superior being, the man
whose remarkable will power had been enough to save
him."

"It's incredible," I murmured.

"Wait, that isn't all," replied N. "Naturally I ran
through all my money. The house in New York and the
house in the country both had gone the way of the
bottles I'd drunk. And my children didn't go to fancy
schools any more. I'd nothing left to feed my family
with. I had to fall back on shameless borrowing, 'touch-
ing' my friends in the way of confirmed alcoholics; lies,
near swindling. . . .

"Then, in spite of my reluctance and my feeling of
intellectual superiority, I began to wonder whether Alcoholics Anonymous couldn't do something for me. I

◇◇

went to one of their meetings. And there I did in fact make a strange discovery. The people around me were certainly not intellectuals. But I shared with even the simplest and least educated of them a common denominator that I couldn't find elsewhere: it was the problem of alcoholism, and our earnest, desperate desire to solve it.

"I left that meeting in a disturbed frame of mind. It didn't prevent my going back into the madhouse four more times. Yes, four times—which brought the number of my cures in less than two years up to nineteen. And all because a successful, rich, happy novelist had drunk *just one* glass of beer in blissful Bermuda."

N. was still smiling. Was he smiling at himself? Or at the horror he realized his story was arousing in me? Whatever it was, he went on:

"The nineteenth time they shut me up, after treatment and sedatives had restored my reason, I took a good look at the lunatics around me. And I said to myself: 'You've got to be honest with yourself once and for all and stop deceiving yourself that it's pure chance you keep coming here. If you go on drinking, you'll spend the rest of your life among these people and others like them.'

"When I left the hospital, the first thing I did was to join one of the groups of Alcoholics Anonymous. And my problem was solved. I've lost my self-satisfaction at being an intellectual; I feel I'm among equals and comrades who have suffered as I have, and that our common suffering makes us love each other. I need them

more than they need me. So much so that after years of
sobriety I still go to six meetings a week, beside that of
my own group, whose president I am. And whenever I
have time I go and speak to distant isolated groups of
A. A. all over the States."

"And how do you earn your living?" I asked him.

"Oh, I scrape along. I write for the radio and television. I'm also working—very slowly—on a new book.
We shall see."

The writer wasn't smiling now.

"What really matters," he added, "and this I've learnt
from A. A., is not intelligence, or talent; it's the life of
the spirit."

He got up. He had to leave for Cleveland that afternoon, in order to get to Texas next day.

We crossed the dining room together. Everyone gave
N. a friendly smile as he passed, and many of them
added:

"God bless you."

It wasn't just a polite formula. There was deep sin-
cerity and warmth in their voices. Hearing them, I began to think about the feature of Alcoholics Anonymous
that I found hardest to understand.

X

Games of Chance

The knowledge that one has touched rock bottom; the admission of utter defeat; the fear, horror, and instinctive recoil from one's own nakedness and the empty gulf yawning ahead; the panic-stricken appeal to Alcoholics Anonymous; the immediate help given by the whole association; the extraordinary confidence one alcoholic feels in another, because they talk together as sick men, accomplices, or equals; the power of example (and thence of hope) that the reformed alcoholic gives his miserable brother; the simple and precise rules of behavior he is taught; the unwearying, intelligent, brotherly care lavished on each newcomer by the whole group; the necessity of being ever on guard against some insidious return of the disease—none of this psychological technique is difficult to understand, and one can easily follow step by step the road that leads from complete degradation to the reconquest of oneself.

◇◇

However, the route that has been planned by Alcoholics Anonymous in the course of twenty-five years of unrivaled experience does not end here. It goes further. But now it encroaches upon a region that can only be entered if one has a certain predisposition or aptitude which many people lack, I among them.

It is, in fact, a question of faith. It is a question of believing in a Power superior to mankind and alone able to safeguard the alcoholic's future.

For, according to the doctrine of Alcoholics Anonymous, human help, however generous, understanding, and devoted, is not enough. It can, of course, awaken the alcoholic's desire to be delivered from his addiction, and the courage he needs; it can show the way, support his first steps, and give him back his sobriety. But the disease is so virulent and has so profoundly affected his organs, nerves, and brain that the threat is only suspended, never finally eliminated. It will be there, crouching on the watch, all his life.

The passage of time and the force of habit diminish and weaken the effect of human help. Also, the reformed alcoholic begins to forget his past struggles; he has gained confidence, found a job, and returned to his old place in society. He has come out of his cocoon. He will have to deal with the usual problems, emotional shocks, grief, wounds to self-esteem, financial difficulties, or troubles in love. If he finds the test too harsh and cruel, he will immediately think of the old remedy. It is poisonous, but effective.

If he is alone with this physical temptation, the ob-

◇◇◇

session he has in the very marrow of his bones, he will give in to it some time or another. Fatally.

And it's impossible that there should be another member of Alcoholics Anonymous always at his side, day and night. Even the best and most watchful nurses leave their patients sometimes, if only for a moment. That moment can be deadly. "One glass, only one, just one." And the alcoholic is hurled back into hell after years of abstinence.

There is only one guardianship which never sleeps, day and night, which protects him from himself to the end of his days; for it comes from no human source—it is derived from a Superior, a Divine, Power.

The practical and psychological methods taught by Alcoholics Anonymous are merely preparations, accessory rules of conduct. True safety is to be found elsewhere. It depends on recognition of a Superior Power, on feeling His presence within one and submitting to His sovereign will.

Of course, the founders and pioneers of Alcoholics Anonymous were not led to this spiritual conclusion by means of argument, deduction, or proof. The opposite was the case. Bill W. was saved from limbo, snatched from the jaws of death, by a moment of revelation. Everything has come from that. Yet when Bill W. tried to share his marvelous discovery with other alcoholics, he failed absolutely and in the most lamentable fashion. He realized then that he must reverse the process, start with trivial earthly human matters and only pass later on to the awareness of divinity. Time and a remarkable success have shown the accuracy of his calculations.

Everything possible has been done, it's true, to make the approach as simple and easy as possible, to win over minds averse to dogma, formality of thought, and the traditional and conventional discipline of established religion.

"Appeal to a Superior Power, however you may conceive of it," say Alcoholics Anonymous. "Jehovah or Allah, Jesus or Buddha, you may choose whichever you like and think of God however you please. The only thing that matters is that you should believe in a Force outside yourself to which you can appeal for help.

"You cannot do without superhuman help. To safeguard your sobriety you must reform your whole character. You must lay aside envy, pride, unsociability, hypersensitivity, and anxiety. Your alcoholism isn't an isolated and independent disease. It is bound up with all these character traits. You are destroying yourself with drink so as to exalt or benumb, satisfy or forget them. While they exist, you will always be in danger.

"You cannot achieve this inner change by yourself. Therefore, you must realize your innate need of a Superior Power, *of whatever kind,* so long as you can put your trust in It.

"And if, even under these conditions, your mind rejects the idea of divinity, then you must take our free confraternity as your Superior Power. It is certainly wiser than you, reckoning by experience, number of members, and the sum total of their suffering. And when you are overcome by weakness, indecision, or exhaustion, call on the group spirit, with its collective strength, to support and guide your failing courage."

This is the gist of the *Credo* of Alcoholics Anonymous. It is expressed in a splendid slogan:

> May God give me enough serenity of mind to accept things which cannot be changed,
> Enough courage to change things which are in my power to change,
> And wisdom enough to recognize the difference betwcen the two.

Next come "The Twelve Steps," a list of the spiritual stages that an alcoholic must pass through, one by one, if he wants to ensure his physical and mental regeneration. The first consists of realizing his own inability to dominate his craving and govern his own life. The second, of believing that a Superior Power can save him. The third, of deciding to put his will and life in God's hands, "however he may conceive of Him."

Thus, mounting one step after another (an inventory of his misdeeds and faults; prayers to God—again "however he may conceive of Him"—to chastise him; confession of his sins; meditation, to strengthen his contact with divinity), the alcoholic arrives at the twelfth and last stage, where he is told:

"Having reached the top of the twelve steps, and having arrived at a state of spiritual awakening, we must pass on this message to other alcoholics and apply these principles to everything we do."

It must be thoroughly understood that these precepts

◇◇◇

do not represent an essential catechism; they are not in any sense a list of commandments. Whenever they appear in one of the publications of Alcoholics Anonymous, they are referred to as "The Twelve Suggested Steps."

I repeat, there is nothing obligatory, nothing rigid about this extraordinarily tolerant association: no subscription, no entry blanks, no expulsion, not even religious belief. A perfect example of this can be found in a book published by Alcoholics Anonymous under the title: *Twelve Steps and Twelve Traditions*.

One of the groups had welcomed a new member called Eddie A., a commercial traveler. He soon proved himself one of the best of their recruits. Happy and proud of his conversion to abstinence and his return to health, he put all his energy, powers of persuasion, persistence, and the personal magnetism that had made him a successful salesman of automobile varnish, into helping other alcoholics in their struggle upward from the depths. In fact, no one could have carried out the instructions of the twelfth step—to help one's neighbor— with more zeal and detachment.

But there was one thing lacking. Eddie A. was an unbeliever. Absolutely, obstinately, and aggressively. The notion of help from a Superior Power seemed to him not only inadmissible but detrimental to the spirit animating Alcoholics Anonymous.

"We would get along far better without this absurd idea about God," he used to say every week to fellow members of his group.

Now, these people were deeply religious, so much so that, since their purpose in life was to rescue as many alcoholics as possible, they went so far as to hope that Eddie A. would be punished for his blasphemies by a serious relapse.

But Eddie A. remained maddeningly sober. Then his turn came to address the open meeting.

The other members looked forward to his speech with alarm. They guessed what would happen, and they were right. Eddie A. paid striking homage to Alcoholics Anonymous and eloquently described the joy he had derived from carrying out the twelfth step, but he added vehemently:

"But I can't take all this pious stuff. It's just mush for the feeble-minded. This group doesn't need that sort of thing. To hell with it all!"

The audience rose to its feet, horrified and furious.

"Get out! Get out!" they shouted as one man.

The veteran members took Eddie A. to one side and said to him:

"You have no right to talk that way here. You must either stop saying that sort of thing or quit."

"Is that so?" asked Eddie sarcastically.

He went to a bookcase and took out several printed leaflets. They were copies of the preface of the first book published by the association, containing its fundamental principles: *Alcoholics Anonymous*.

Eddie turned the pages for a moment and then read aloud:

"The only necessary condition for membership of A. A. is an honest desire to stop drinking."

Eddie waved the paper he was holding.

"Well, boys," he demanded, "when you wrote these words, did you mean them or not?"

The "old timers" exchanged glances in silence. They were beaten. Eddie remained a member of their group.

This happened in 1938, when the association was only three years old and was still feeling its way and looking for guiding principles. Afterwards, there was a considerable advance towards tolerance. Today such a question couldn't arise.

I have more than once heard agnostics or indomitable atheists defend their views freely and calmly in private meetings of Alcoholics Anonymous, when personal problems were under discussion.

Yet the truth is that such cases are rare. Belief in a Superior Power—however conceived of—is to be found in most members of Alcoholics Anonymous. And is it really surprising? A paralysed man who has been carried into the grotto of Lourdes on a stretcher and walks out seems to radiate faith, even if he had been full of doubt or incredulity when he arrived. And every member of Alcoholics Anonymous who remembers the days of his downfall and sees himself restored to life likewise feels he has been to some degree the object of a miracle.

And then . . . and then . . . there are strange clashes between a man and his destiny, when some un-

foreseen and unforeseeable event changes the orienta-
tion of his whole life. Some think of it as a game of
chance; others, as a sign of Providence. Isn't this last
interpretation likely to be the one chosen by the dying
man who touches the hand of a healer or the drowning
sailor who sees a sail coming to his rescue just when he
is exhausted and giving up hope?

Because of the very nature of his personal tragedy,
the vicissitudes of his downfall, and his struggle to arise
from it, because of the obscure forces (favorable or disastrous) that have rolled him ceaselessly back and
forth in their ebb and flow, nearly every member of
Alcoholics Anonymous has been faced at some time
with one of these critical "chances," these decisive "co-
incidences."

I have been told two curious stories about them.

In a long, gray, melancholy street near Eighth Avenue stood the oldest among the association's clubs,
founded when Alcoholics Anonymous was only just beginning to take shape. It consisted of one small, low,
poor room, very sketchily furnished.

A. A. groups had met there for twenty years. Innumerable public confessions had been made there,
each one a terrible real-life story. Hundreds of alcoholics—both men and women—had rediscovered their
dignity and joy of life there, after being saved from utter ruin. Its paneled walls were worn with age and
seemed to have a patina derived from poverty, patience,
and effort.

◇◇◇

I was there one evening with Bob, the *Herald Tribune* reporter who had been my devoted and most valuable guide from the first day of my investigation and who had quickly become my friend.

The meeting had just come to an end in the usual way, with a short prayer repeated by the audience standing. I was still not used to this custom, and my face must have shown as much. Bob said to me with a tranquil smile:

"I know, I know! I was logical, critical, and agnostic myself once. Then one day there I was in the abyss, crying out for help, like most other A. A. members. . . ."

After the meeting was over, people were drinking coffee as usual, talking about their problems and affairs or simply about the fine weather or the rain. A tall fellow passing by with an empty cup in his hand stopped for a moment.

"Hello, Bob!" he said.

"Hello, Burt!" said Bob—and his deep-set eyes shone with a sudden warmth. "How are you doing?"

"Just fine," said Burt.

He went off to the end of the room, where an enormous coffeepot was steaming. His broad athletic shoulders, broken nose, and flattened ears attracted my attention from the first; later, during the prayer, it was the concentrated earnestness of his rugged face.

"Who's Burt?" I asked Bob.

I thought I noticed a mischievous glint in my friend's eyes, but it was only for a moment.

◇◇◇

"He'll carry the marks of his first profession with him
for life," said Bob. "Burt was a boxer, a very fine boxer.
Powerful, quick, aggressive. He would have gone far if
he hadn't begun drinking. But having this constitutional
predisposition, or allergy, we all suffer from, he became
a champion alcoholic and nothing else. That was the
end of the ring and his dreams of fame."

I took a look at the ex-pugilist. He had put one of his
muscular arms around the shoulders of a thin old
man and was laughing with him like a child. Bob
went on:

"Like every alcoholic who has no definite profession,
Burt took various small ill-paid jobs to get money for
drink. Fired from one after the other, he ended up
working for a plasterer. He stuck at that longer than at
anything else. His boss was very lenient. That was when
I got to know Burt: he came to do a job in my house.
You saw what an attractive mug he has when he laughs.
I took a fancy to the boy at once, and of course I soon
realized that he was a confirmed alcoholic. I told him
about A. A., without pressing the point, just to drop a
hint that he could come to me if he wanted the association's help."

"What did he say?" I asked.

"He pretended not to hear," said Bob. "But I saw him
six months later. His boss had fired him at last. He had
just got married to a young woman who had accepted
him and loved him just as he was, in spite of fits of
drunkenness, outrageous brawls, and nights spent in
prison. And, great strapping bully though he was, he

couldn't earn enough for her to live on. He was ready to try almost anything, even Alcoholics Anonymous. He had touched rock bottom, as we say."

Burt went by again with his empty cup.

"Hello, Bob," he said.

"Hello, Burt," said Bob.

Once more the light of friendship shone in his eyes.

"I went to see Burt's boss," he said. "He was a very good sort, and what was more, he had heard about Alcoholics Anonymous. I told him I would be Burt's godfather and mentor. He agreed to take him back."

Bob went off to get himself some coffee. When he returned, he resumed his story:

"At first Burt had his ups and downs, as we all do. And even one or two relapses. But on the whole it wasn't too tough for him. His feeling for his wife helped him a lot. And then one fine day, after three years, yes, three whole years of keeping sober, he suddenly decided to go and get drunk. He knew perfectly well what it meant: the hellish cycle starting all over again, no work, the gutter, prison, and probably a break with his wife. But nothing mattered to him any more. He stopped at the first bar he came to and drank glass after glass till he passed out."

"But why? Whatever for?"

Bob gave a slight smile in which his eyes had no part. He said slowly:

"I know from our talks together that you've drunk a lot in the course of your life, and often much too much. But you're lucky enough not to be a true, constitutional alcoholic. So you can't know, or even imagine what it's like to have a terrible, sudden return of a craving you thought had grown less or been altogether destroyed by years of abstinence. The old disease suddenly comes to life inside you like some cunning animal in its cage. There it is, begging, weeping, howling, insisting. . . ."

Bob was silent for a few moments. Then his usual firm but gentle expression returned.

"A man—especially an alcoholic—always needs an excuse for doing something he knows he shouldn't," he said. "Burt was no exception to the rule. When he decided to get drunk—and ruin his life—he had a very good reason.

"It was an ordinary Sunday morning. Burt had slept late. His wife had been to church. About eleven o'clock Burt went to the delicatessen on the corner to buy something for lunch—as he did every Sunday. But this time he got the feeling—whether justified or imaginary, it doesn't matter—that everyone was unfriendly or sneering at him. And he knew only too well why this was. He had lived in this part of town since long before his marriage, and when he took to drink they had all known him as a ragged, quarrelsome, obscene beggar. This particular Sunday, it seemed to Burt they were all remembering that time—tradesmen he had owed money to, men he had beaten up (taking advantage of his strength and boxer's training), and women he had treated like prostitutes.

"Burt went back home, threw his purchases on the

kitchen table, and said to himself: 'So it's no use leading a model life for three years! In spite of all my efforts, to *them* I'm still a brute. Very well, I'll show *them. They* asked for it.'

"Burt thrust his weekly pay into his pocket and was already imagining the bar sparkling with glasses; the smell, taste, and blissful burning warmth of the first whisky; the fieriness of the second; and the escape from life the next whiskies—all the whiskies in the world— would bring him.

"Just then there was a knock at the door. Burt opened it with his fists clenched, ready to knock the intruder downstairs. Three little boys were standing there. Their faces had a scrubbed, Sunday-best look, and they were dressed as boy scouts.

" 'What the hell are you doing here?' growled Burt.

"He only thought of the children as an obstacle between his craving and the drink itself, and he pushed them roughly aside, saying:

" 'I'm in a hurry. I'm going out. . . .'

"But the eldest of the boys, who was about ten, caught hold of his sleeve.

" 'Please, Mr. Burt,' he said, 'our scoutmaster sent us to ask if you'd be our gym instructor.'

" 'What?' stammered Burt. 'What did you say, Ed?'

"The child repeated his question. Burt had to lean against the wall, he suddenly felt so faint.

" 'Don't you want to?' Ed asked.

" 'We were all counting on you, Mr. Burt,' exclaimed the other two boy scouts.

" 'Wait a minute, wait a minute, kids,' said Burt hoarsely. 'Me, gym instructor? . . . But you must know . . . or anyway your parents do . . . what I've been, the things I've done. . . .'

"At that moment he remembered vividly and in horrifying detail how he had knocked out the father of the smallest of the three boys—Dave, whose well-scrubbed, freckled face was now raised to his; and how he had insulted Al's mother, the shopkeeper's wife, because she had refused to go on giving him liquor on credit; and how he had broken up the bar kept by Ed's uncle, before collapsing on the pavement dead drunk and being picked up by the police.

"But the three boy scouts answered in unison:

" 'We only know one thing, Mr. Burt: everyone in the neighborhood thinks we couldn't have a better instructor than you.'

" 'Then—oh well, then—it's agreed, boys,' said Burt. 'See you soon!'

"He shut the door quickly. So as to cry in comfort, cry with remorse and happiness. He was saved. . . ."

While I was trying to imagine that brutal, scarred face stained with tears, Bob made a sign to Burt. The ex-boxer came toward his sponsor.

"I've just been telling our French friend the story of your boy scouts," said Bob.

"Those blessed kids," said Burt softly.

A fanatical, almost ecstatic light shone in his eyes, framed by his shattered brow and broken nose.

"Those blessed kids," he repeated.

He went back to his friends around the coffeepot.

"He really had good luck," I said to Bob.

"Luck?" said my friend. "Maybe. I see it as something else."

He suddenly began to laugh, and added:

"Anyhow I warn you not to use that word when you talk to Burt. Reformed though he is, he might knock you down. . . ."

It was a dark night.

A wet wind lashed Battery Park, the prow of the island which shelters the harbor of New York, the largest in the world. Docks, avenues, and skyscrapers were distinguishable by the patterns their lights made. Farther off, a dim reflection on a vast moving surface revealed the presence of the infinite, solitary, eternal ocean.

I had a little time to kill. I wandered at random along the piers and docks, fascinated by the potent charm of all great harbors. Liners covered in lights like stars, sleeping freighters watched over by a single lamp, gigantic wharves, sailors' bars, oilskins varnished by rain.

At length I reached the building I was heading for. It was tall and massive, like an enormous rectangular fortress, and took up the whole of one block, with roads on all four sides. In spite of the lateness of the hour, there were lights shining from hundreds of windows all along the façade and right up to the roof. The pediment over the huge porch bore the inscription:

◇◇◇

SEAMEN'S CHURCH INSTITUTE
OF NEW YORK

As soon as I had crossed the threshold, I was completely lost. The dimensions of the hall were as vast as
those of some enormous railroad station, the movement and noise as lively, and the approaches, passages,
and stairs as numerous. There were voices speaking in
every accent in the world, faces tanned by every sea
wind; and the pitch and swell of every ocean was in the
rolling gait of these men. Most of them carried sailors'
duffel bags on their shoulders.

This time I was without a guide or companion. Unexpectedly discovering a few hours earlier that I had
nothing to do this evening, I looked in the little yellow
booklet to see which meetings of Alcoholics Anonymous
took place on Thursdays. There were more than sixty.
But I was attracted particularly by one of them—
first because it was clearly a meeting of a sailors' group,
and also because the notice was followed by the words:
"Men Only."

Most meetings of Alcoholics Anonymous took place in
a club or hall in the district, or in a room attached to a
church but meant for secular use and easy to find. But
it was different in the Seamen's Church Institute.
Around and above the immense hall swarming with
sailors were thousands of rooms, occupying fifteen stories, each room with its own special purpose.

How was I to find, in this colossal beehive, the one
cell that housed the meeting of the sailors' A. A. every
Thursday?

❖❖❖❖❖❖❖❖❖❖❖❖❖❖❖❖❖❖❖❖❖❖❖❖❖❖❖❖❖❖❖❖❖❖❖❖❖❖❖

I stood hesitating for quite a while in the middle of a rough, sturdy crowd, continually dispersing along different corridors and staircases but as quickly reassembling. At last I went up to a gray-haired old man whose black wool jersey moulded his heavily built torso and who was smoking his pipe at a little distance from the crowd.

"Alcoholics Anonymous?" he said slowly, between puffs. "Oh yes . . . sure . . . they've got a room here . . . but where? You'd better look at that bulletin board over there," and he waved his pipe vaguely toward the far end of the hall. "You'll find the A. A. meeting listed there, I guess."

While he was talking, a delicate-looking little man, neatly and plainly dressed, stopped close to us. He said to me:

"The A. A. meeting? I can take you there. I'm going myself. My name is Jim C. and I am an alcoholic."

Jim's clear, thoughtful eyes were already fixed on me with the generous and ready sympathy that all members of Alcoholics Anonymous show toward another alcoholic or anyone interested in their problem.

We crossed the hall and got into an elevator. Our journey was long and crowded. There was plenty of time for Jim C. to tell me that he was born in Cork in Ireland, and for me to describe my first assignment as a reporter in that same town, in the far-off heroic days when it was the rampart of resistance against British rule, and when its Lord Mayor was dying on a hunger strike in a London prison. Jim C. listened with eyes half-closed, as if to a passage from the Bible. Then he said simply:

"I have a house there. It's yours, whenever you like."

The elevator took us up to the floor where the sea-faring A. A. group was collecting. I remember the peculiar character of those meetings very well.

"Why don't you allow women in, when they come to all the other meetings?" I asked Jim C.

He chuckled, and began explaining as we walked along a corridor with a great many numbered doors in it:

"You ought to understand, if you knew Cork in the days of its greatness.

"A lot of alcoholic sailors who come to our group—a really enormous number of them—come from Ireland. Southern Ireland, of course, free, Catholic Ireland. Well, the president's an Irishman, too, but from the North, where they're still faithful to the English crown. What's more, he's a Protestant. . . ."

I remembered the fanatical passions, both political and religious, which had torn Ireland in half during her war for independence, and that the fire they left behind has never been extinguished. . . .

"In fact," I said, "your president is a heretic and a renegade to the other Irish."

"Exactly," said Jim C. "And you can imagine what sort of language he gets from the new Irish members, who generally arrive drunk at their first meeting. . . ."

Jim C. chuckled more softly still, and went on:

"They settle down in the end. Things always have to settle down in A. A., because the only thing that mat-

◇◇

ters is that everyone should stick together against the common trouble. But to start with—Christ! the greatest expert in obscenity would learn something new!"

Jim C. stopped at one of the hundred identical doors, and said with a disarmingly boyish smile, a real Irish smile:

"That's why we don't want any ladies at our meetings."

However, the meeting that followed was conducted with perfect decency and an austere and simple dignity.

A dozen or so sailors were sitting at a round table in a room hung with pictures and engravings of the sea and ships. Even if I hadn't known their calling in advance, I would have guessed it at once. Traces of their life on the open sea were to be seen in their faces, their movements, and the depth of their gaze.

And even if Jim C. hadn't introduced me to the president of the group when we went in, I would have unhesitatingly picked him out as the captain of his side. He was nearing sixty but was so full of vitality, so strong physically, and so confident in hearing and gestures that he seemed to defy old age. He had a magnificent face, lean and clean cut, with a profile like that on a coin. He talked in the simplest, most natural way possible, but his voice, like his expression, commanded immediate attention. The authority he imposed was spontaneous. He was made to be an organizer and leader.

"My name is William F.," the president told me, "but please call me Bill, like everyone else. Okay? Sit anywhere you like. The meeting is now open."

I sat down some way from the table, the better to

see the men sitting around it. This meeting wasn't in the least like the others I had been to, numerous and varied though they had been. There was no platform, and no audience, and no one stood up and told the story of his life. That would have been unnecessary. The seamen gathered here this evening had all known each other for a long time. They had roughed it at sea, drunk, and toiled together.

Most of them were in the prime of life, broad-shouldered and with rugged features. It must have taken an enormous amount of drink—and such drink, too!—to induce men like these to cry for mercy, and to make them seek out Alcoholics Anonymous. How many times had they missed a sailing, been turned out of work, got into brawls in some bar, and awakened lying on the pavement in some alley close to the waterfront. Those dreadful times had marked them all in one way or another: slight tremors of the head, red patches on the skin, chronic laryngitis, restless movements of their heavy hands.

But their eyes were clear and their expressions serene.

They spoke in turn, beginning with the man sitting on the president's right and going all around the table. There was nothing ideological or emotional about their remarks. Slowly and deliberately they suggested practical and trivial methods, all drawn from their own long experience, of fighting the craving for alcohol, exacerbated as it was by life at sea and the temptations of ports. One of them described his loneliness, another his longing for land, another his jealousy of his wife, and another the vanity that made him want to show he could "take it" as well as his matoo.

All of them supported their arguments with one of Alcoholics Anonymous' basic principles or with a recollection of a difficult voyage or a call at some far-off port.

The round-table conference was almost at an end. The only ones who had not yet taken part were two sailors sitting on William F.'s right. They were very young and remarkably like each other—not in actual features, or in that air of belonging to the same family which a common calling often gives. They both had the same hollow cheeks and narrow shoulders, and above all the same anxious, guilty expressions, lit by timid, incredulous hope. They were "newcomers," still saturated with drink; it was as if they had been flayed and the new skin they were growing was still delicate and vulnerable.

"Well, it's your turn now," William F. said gently but firmly.

Then the two boys timidly and hesitantly described their ordeals. Their experiences had been almost identical, though they had never sailed together. They had dreamed of the sea since childhood and signed on at the first opportunity. But life aboard ship had been tougher than they had expected. No mistake or clumsiness was ever passed over by officers or other seamen. It was an arduous, rough, coarse, hostile world. They began drinking to forget their troubles and also to show that they

were men. They got a taste for it immediately, but their
physical tolerance was poor. This only made them want
it more. Young as they were, they had both missed their
ships more than once and awakened in brothels after
days of unconsciousness, without their money and
sometimes without their clothes. They had begun to
feel afraid of themselves, and since they had heard
people talking about A. A.—here they were.

"What do you say, boys?" William F. asked the others.

The veteran seamen and alcoholics talked to the
young men with a kindly interest that was curiously
moving, coming from such rough-looking characters
and expressed in such harsh tones. Each of them had
his own system or trick to suggest; but they all agreed
that the essential thing was to keep in contact with
other sailor members of A. A.

"Write here," they said. "You'll get an answer every
time. If we're at sea, our mates'll do it. And whenever
you put into port, go straight to the group there. You'll
find one everywhere. Bill here'll give you the list."

The two boys listened to the old salts, the veteran
drunks, with the expressions of attentive, admiring students.

The meeting came to an end. They all left.

"Excuse me a moment," William F. said to me, "I've
got some papers to sign. Jim'll keep you company. And
there's some coffee left."

I questioned my friend from Cork about his next
voyage.

"I don't go to sea often nowadays," he said. "I'm busy

rescuing drunks. It's work that's well worth doing. I may go back to Ireland soon."

"And what about the old days?" I asked.

"Oh yes—I've been a rolling stone. . . ," said Jim.

He mentioned the names of several far-off ports that I happened to know, and many others that I had never visited. I tried to get him to talk about these, but he shook his head and said:

"I can't tell you anything, nothing at all. I didn't see anything. I stopped at the first bar, and there I stayed till my ship sailed."

"Everywhere?" I exclaimed.

"Everywhere."

In other words, at Hong Kong and Rio de Janeiro, Shanghai and Valparaiso, Rangoon and Tahiti. Jim had been to all of them, but blind to their color, deaf to their songs, and unaware of their odors.

"It's the same with all alcoholic sailors," said Jim.

"But how did you manage to stop drinking?" I asked.

The little Irishman from the South pointed to the door through which the big Irishman from the North had gone, and said:

"Bill. It was him. He found me on the pier at San Francisco. I was just a tramp then, and I touched him for a dollar. Next day I got another off him to buy liquor. Then we talked a bit, you know, as sailor to sailor, or alcoholic to alcoholic."

"So that Bill . . . he's another . . . ," I murmured, mostly to myself.

The fact was, in spite of all my research, it hadn't

till then entered my head that William F. (with his perfect health, his natural authority and leadership) must—as president of the group—have been an alcoholic once himself.

Soon afterwards Bill returned. Jim left us together.

"I'm afraid I was longer than I expected," William F. said. "There's no end to all this paper work."

"All of it for Alcoholics Anonymous?" I asked.

William F. looked at me in astonishment; then he burst out laughing, and answered:

"Certainly it's for A. A.! I'm in charge of the whole department dealing with 'sailors in transit' in this building. And do you know what that means? Last year the Seamen's Institute provided lodgings for more than 230,000 men; I handled more than 70,000 pieces of luggage and served about 900,000 meals."

He rattled off the figures, quickly, clearly, and proudly. Under this avalanche I had only one thought: this magnificent-looking man who does so much and carries such a heavy burden of responsibility, can he really once have been a sailor demoralized by drink?

"Tell me, Bill," I said abruptly, "of course you were once an alcoholic, but how bad were you?"

"So bad," William F. replied in clear tones, meeting my eyes frankly and with dignity, "that I've seen nothing like it in any of the men you've met here, though God knows. . . ."

He made an eloquent gesture, and went on:

"I was chief engineer, and one of the best, as I don't mind saying now that it doesn't matter any more. I sailed all the great rivers and lakes in this country and after that the seven seas—drinking more and more all the time. I was chucked out of the merchant marine for drunkenness. Then came the war. I was chucked out of the navy for drunkenness. We call it 'dishonorable discharge.' And I landed in the Bowery among ragged lousy tramps and beggars.

"Then I had some luck. I found somewhere to live. It was the cellar of a tumble-down house, and the owner let me stay there on condition that I see to the ancient boiler down there. Fine end to the career of a chief engineer, and one of the best, wasn't it?

"Well, I deserved nothing better. I had reached the lowest depths of degradation and collapse. All I had to wear in the dead of winter was a disgustingly dirty pair of jeans, a ragged jersey, and a pair of worn-out, gaping shoes. I had forgotten the point of soap or razor. I hardly ever ate. And what stuff when I did! Anything I could make out of miserable odd jobs or begging I spent on drink. And what drink! I was covered with sores and vermin. But I didn't care about anything, so long as I got my drink."

William F. was still looking me straight in the face. I shut my eyes for a moment, to try to picture the vital, fine-looking man I was talking to as a sordid, hideous tramp.

"Well, one winter morning," William F. went on, "I was lying there in my rags on the floor of the cellar, close to the boiler, for it was appallingly cold. The wind came in through the broken panes of the air vent, and a little wan daylight also. All around me was rubbish and filth of every description, dumped in the cellar by the neighbors. I was feeling ghastly. I'd not had a drop to drink for two days, no hope of a job, and I hadn't a cent.

"Suddenly a bundle of paper hit me in the face and woke me from my bestial stupor. It was an old magazine, thrown away by a passer-by as if into an ash can. It had lost its cover, but I opened it and turned the pages mechanically. Then, without knowing why, I began to take a vague, muddled interest. Something I found in its pages seemed to be addressed to me personally, or else the author was talking about me.

"That tattered magazine which had landed on my dirty face was the number of *The Saturday Evening Post* containing Jack Alexander's report on Alcoholics Anonymous. You know what an important article it was. . . ."

"I do indeed," I said. "It was the first time a weekly with an enormous circulation had written about Alcoholics Anonymous. That article was a great event in the development of the association."

"Exactly," said William F. "But it took me all day to read it. The light was bad in the cellar, and I had gone half blind as a result of drink. When I reached the last line, I thought to myself: perhaps there's something for me, too, in all that.

"Now at that time the A. A. organization in its present form, with its groups and intergroups and telephone numbers, simply didn't exist. The only means of getting in touch with them was a post-office box number, which Jack Alexander quoted at the end of his article. To send them a letter I had to beg a piece of paper, an envelope, and a stamp off my landlord.

◇◇◇

"Next day, a man—an alcoholic—arrived in my cellar. He talked to me a long time; then he gave me the address of a little club where A. A. members met."

A curiously tender smile softened William F.'s mouth, visually so firm as to be almost stern. He said gently:

"The club on 24th Street."

I knew it well. I had been there only the evening before, hearing how Burt the ex-boxing champion was saved from a fatal relapse by the providential arrival of three boy scouts.

William F. went on:

"To go to the club I had to borrow again from the landlord of the house whose cellar I lived in. I hadn't the money for my subway fare. . . ."

William F. got up and expanded his broad chest. His face was full of strength, energy, and serenity.

"My return to life began in that club," he said. "And now, here I am. . . ."

With a wide gesture he swept away the walls of the room and took in the whole of the huge building where he controlled the fate of thousands and thousands of sailors from all over the world.

"You're a happy man," I told William F.

For the first time I saw signs of weakness and a sort of disunity in that face, which normally seemed immune to fatigue and discouragement.

It was only for a brief moment, and William F.'s voice was clear and firm as he replied:

"No. I'm not happy. I'm paying—through my daughter. She's twenty-eight years old, and as good as a stranger to me. My wife wanted it that way—she was

◇◇

my wife at the time I took to drink. She was a German by birth and a woman of relentlessly rigid principles. From the first time I took too much I became a marked man for her, despicable, as good as dead. That's how she brought up our daughter. All the letters I wrote the child were destroyed unread. At last, three years ago, I heard that my daughter was teaching in a college in the Middle West. I went to see her. Nothing much came of it. All the same, I was with her, and she probably saw that I was different from the man her mother had described. . . ."

William F. was silent; then he took a clipping from a local paper out of his wallet. It was a photograph of a beautiful, serene-looking girl who had won some university honors. William F. studied it for some time, then carefully folded it up again.

"Yes, I'm paying dearly," he said. "And it's only right I should. Providence has done enough for me already by sending that old copy of *The Saturday Evening Post* into my sordid cellar and dropping it on my filthy mug, to save me from destruction."

When I got outside, I wandered along the sea front for a while. I thought of Burt and the three little boys who *chanced* to ring his bell at the crucial moment. I thought of William F. and what would have become of him if a passer-by hadn't *chanced* to throw a battered old magazine through the air vent of his cellar.

Some sea gulls drifted out of the night sky and settled on the invisible waves like pieces of white paper, undecipherable pages from the book of fate.

XI

Green Light

She was about forty years old, and her charming face was gentle and delicate but full of energy. Pinned to the right shoulder of her smart dark dress, she wore an exquisite pale-colored flower.

"I am Doris H.," she told me, "chief secretary of Intergroup."

Alcoholics Anonymous have established an organization with this name in all the larger towns and cities in the United States. Open every day, even Sundays and holidays, its function is to receive appeals from alcoholics at the end of their tether (or from their frantic families) and to provide immediate help. The most important of them, the New York branch, was run by the slender attractive woman with the flower on her shoulder who was now receiving me.

I was once again face to face with the paradox I had several times encountered in the course of my strange journey through the world of Alcoholics Anony-

mous. The person I was talking to was evidently well
equipped physically, intellectually, and spiritually for
the extremely heavy responsibility she had to carry.
And yet I knew without any possibility of a doubt that
since she belonged to Alcoholics Anonymous and held
an important post there, she must at some time of her
life have been a wreck, ravaged and brutalized by
drink.

There was no need for Doris H. to tell me her life
story; I knew this to be so. I had only to remember
Eve M., in charge of public relations; or William F., director of the department for Sailors in Transit in the
vast Seamen's Institute; or John M., who presided over
the meetings in the Bowery; or Bill W., founder, pio-
neer, and organizer of Alcoholics Anonymous. All had
once been tramps or had been confined in prisons or
mental homes.

"I'm entirely at your service," said Doris H. "But I
think the best thing you can do is to look, listen, and ask
whatever questions you like. Make yourself at home."

"I will indeed," I said.

"Good luck," said Doris H. smiling.

She bent over the forms, plans, graphs, and leaflets
spread out over the top of her huge desk. As she moved,
a tremulous gleam was thrown onto the petals of the
flower on her shoulder; for Doris H. was sitting close
to the air vent, which was the only source of daylight
the room possessed.

The New York Intergroup had its premises in a basement reached by a few steps leading down from East

39th Street, a busy, crowded, noisy, depressing, and distinctly dirty thoroughfare much like so many others in parts of Manhattan. It consisted of a room running the whole length of the building and another, much smaller one furnished with three dilapidated armchairs and opening on to a tiny garden containing one stunted tree.

Like all Alcoholics Anonymous' offices, it was modest to the verge of poverty. But here, too, the activity and efficiency were astonishing.

Besides Doris H., busy among her documents and files on a slightly elevated platform, there were four people—a woman and three men—sitting at four separate tables.

The woman—gray hair, glasses, austere clothes and face—was manipulating a small telephone switchboard opposite Doris H.'s platform. One of the men sat at a table covered with a green cloth in the middle of the room. He had a bony head and rather haggard eyes set in a cadaverous unhealthy face, and he was slightly hunchbacked.

Two other tables with green cloths stood one on either side of the door leading to the smaller room, the room with the shabby armchairs and the sad little garden. At the table on the right sat a charming white-haired old man radiating good nature, gentleness, and wisdom. His neighbor, on the other hand, was a very large man with athletic shoulders and torso, a straight neck and a firm chin, and a frank, courageous, and cheerful expression. In spite of the silver hair at his temples, he looked remarkably young and carefree, and his manliness immediately inspired sympathy and confidence in other men.

He was the one I instinctively chose to approach.

When I introduced myself, I was greeted with a broad smile in keeping with his countenance.

"Fine," he said, "I'm a journalist, too. On the *Daily News*. My name's Arthur H., but we're both in the same racket, so you might as well call me Art."

He filled his pipe. I sat down opposite him; there was a telephone between us on the table.

"Well, you know my profession already," Art went on. "The woman at the switchboard is a hospital nurse. The hunchback keeps accounts in a saloon bar. The nice old guy is an elevator operator in a hotel."

"And you all work here for nothing?" I asked.

"All, always," said Art. "Except Doris, of course. She's on the permanent staff of A. A. It's her regular job, all the year round. The others spare what time they can from their jobs, free time, and families."

"And how about you?" I asked him.

"I come here every Thursday," said Art. "It's my day off from the paper."

"Yet you're married," I said, pointing to his wedding ring.

"Oh, my present wife understands that, all right," said Art with a broad smile. "She's an A. A. member, too."

Art slowly lit his pipe; then between two puffs he said:

"As for our system, it's childishly simple. You see

those three electric bulbs over the switchboard operator's head: white, red, and green? Each color corresponds to one of the tables; the green light is mine. When the telephone rings, I look up. If the light that goes on is mine, I take the call."

"And then?"

"Then I take down the address of the alcoholic—man or woman—who wants help, and then. . . .

Art got up, stretched his large body, and in two strides stood in front of an immense map of New York which covered all of one wall. The way it had been sectioned off and the little flags pinned on the various segments made it look like a map of military operations: the zones were defined by letters, Q.G., P.C., the names in code.

"I locate the district containing my alcoholic's street on this plan," said Art, "and the corresponding group among all the hundreds in New York. See?"

"I see. And then?"

"Then. . . ."

Art went back to his table, opened the drawer, and took out a book as thick as a telephone directory.

"This book contains the names (classified under groups and days of the week) of all the people—men and women—who are holding themselves in readiness to hurry wherever the person on duty at Intergroup may send them. From that moment the game is in the visitor's hands. All I have to do is make a note of the name, address, and any other details I've been given and hand them to Doris for her files."

"Do you get many calls?" I asked.

"Varies a lot," said Art. "Sometimes there's no end to them. Sometimes it's quiet, like today. Then one has time to chat to the clients who come to see us in person."

Without getting up, Art inclined his long torso sideways into the doorway beside which he was sitting and said loudly to someone in the small room with the battered chairs:

"Come on in, buddy!"

An abject individual detached himself from the depths of one of the armchairs, whose back had concealed him up to now. He staggered towards us, and had to clutch the table for support.

He was an ageless being, perhaps forty, perhaps sixty. A rough beard of an indeterminate shade swallowed up his sunken cheeks. It was impossible to guess the color of his eyes, they were so dim with rheum and darkened by purple veins. His deplorable jacket, buttoned over his bare skin, left his jutting collarbones and scraggy neck exposed.

Art brought up a chair, and the tramp fell back into it. This movement was enough to liberate a revolting smell of sour dirt, unwashed sweat, and the stench of a body whose every cell was impregnated with alcohol.

I held my breath. I was ashamed of showing my repugnance by this reflex action, but I couldn't help it. The poor wretch obviously aroused no disgust in Art, and (stranger still) no pity. All I could read on his face was natural, cheerful good-fellowship.

"How are you? Keeping your end up?" he asked the tramp.

"It's a long job," sighed the man, without opening his lips.

His eyes dropped to his trembling hands, and he said with a pleading smile:

"One little glass would help me through."

Art burst into a loud spontaneous laugh.

"Of course it would, of course. And then another, and another."

"You're right there," said the tramp humbly. "I came here to get cured."

His hands were dancing about on his knees.

I took a packet of cigarettes from my pocket and offered one to our haggard visitor. He seized it with pathetic gratitude and eagerness, and greedily drew in the smoke.

"Don't lose heart, old man," Art said to him. "When I go off duty here, I'll take you to a doctor. He'll disintoxicate you, and then you'll do fine."

"Got no appetite. Can't eat anything," the tramp said.

"Within a week you'll be dreaming about a nice thick steak," said Art.

"A steak—that's no good," said the tramp.

He opened his lips. He hadn't a tooth in his head.

"Well then, a hamburger," said Art gaily.

His loud laugh was infectious. The tramp broke into a series of little chortles and then wiped his bloodshot, tearful eyes with the back of his hand. There was a gleam of hope in his pathetic face. He said:

"I'm really set on it this time, you know. When I left the Bowery this morning, I went around the long way so as not to pass the bar on Second Avenue where I can sometimes get a drink on the cuff."

"I know that bar well," said Art, filling his pipe.

The telephone rang shrilly. The girl at the switchboard answered it, and the white light went on. The bald hunchback took the call and then trotted up with short steps to the vast map of New York. I studied it, too, but for a different reason. I wanted to measure the distance from the Bowery to 39th Street and Intergroup. It was immense.

"You came on foot?" I asked the tramp.

"Certainly," said Art smiling. "If he'd had the money for a subway token, he wouldn't be here but in a bar. A man must be really down and out before he comes to us."

The tramp nodded feebly. I looked him over incredulously: how could this terribly thin, trembling man who had taken no real nourishment for a long time stagger along hour after hour through the huge, swarming, pitiless city?

Art noticed my expression.

"Oh yes," he said, "that's how it is. Where an exhausted, moribund alcoholic like this gets his strength from, I can't imagine, but it seems to be limitless. Why, when I was living in the Bowery. . . ."

"You? No!"

I had blurted out the words unthinkingly, so deeply hurt and shocked was I by the contrast between Art's

handsome, serene, energetic, intelligent face, his
athlete's body, his precious human vitality and warmth,
and the Bowery, the dead end of human beings, the
icy hell of hopeless drunks, shameless beggars, and
ragged hairy phantoms.

Art's laugh rang out louder than ever.

"Why, yes, sure, the Bowery," he said. "Where do
you suppose I went? Every paper in New York had
shown me the door, one after another. Yet I began well
enough. At eighteen I was already a promising reporter.
But I left my promise at the bottom of a bottle, and what
did I do? I became a roomer in the lousy Bowery flophouses, just like him."

Art pointed the bowl of his pipe at the tramp huddled in a chair beside us. Then I understood his attitude
toward the poor wretch: his lack of disgust and pity,
his spontaneous comradeship, his rough offer of help,
the way he joked with him as an equal. And at the same
time I understood why the tramp was so much at ease
with Art, and why he listened to him as one listens to
the voice of hope itself.

"Believe it or not," Art went on, "I was often in worse
physical shape than our pal here. That didn't stop me
walking for miles on the chance of finding drink on
credit, or someone to touch. I particularly remember
one winter day when I crossed this damned city from
side to side, dressed in rags, my shoes full of holes,
nothing in my belly, my eyes gummed together, and all
in a snowstorm and a wind terrible enough to blind ordinary mortals and send them scurrying for shelter."

The telephone rang. The red light went on. The kind old man took the call.

"Next time it'll be me," said Art.

He drew at his pipe placidly, in full command of muscles and nerves. But I was visualizing a tall thin figure dressed in rags staggering from one end of New York to the other, a deluded phantom lashed by the white gusts of a blizzard.

The afternoon was drawing to an end. A dimmer light filtered through the air vent into the basement where the New York Intergroup of Alcoholics Anonymous had its offices.

In this astonishing clearinghouse, signal box, and first-aid station combined (which dealt with appeals for help from drunks at the end of their rope all over this colossal city), it was getting difficult to distinguish the features of the four people who had sacrificed their leisure and rest to come to the rescue: the hospital nurse at her switchboard, and at their respective tables the emaciated, hunchbacked accountant, the charming old elevator man, and lastly Art, the *Daily News* reporter to whom I was talking.

Art threw his large body back in his chair, stretched out a muscular arm, and pressed a button. A bright light went on in the ceiling. The tramp sitting between us suddenly huddled himself in his chair as if someone had hit him in the face, and put his hands over his bloodshot eyes.

Art leaned toward the door beside him and called:

◇◇

"Ben!"

A young man hardly past adolescence came hurrying out of the smaller room, now suddenly dark by contrast. He was extremely thin, and his eyes were shining too brilliantly from their hollow sockets.

"Can I do anything?" he asked eagerly.

"And how!" Art said smilingly. "Take our pal here back to the waiting room. He'll be better off there till I take him to the doctor. And you'll make him some very strong coffee, won't you, and very hot?"

"Sure, Art, sure," said the boy.

He helped the tramp to his feet, and they went out together. Art followed them with his eyes. Then he said:

"You have to give the beginners little tasks to do so that they feel they're already useful and necessary. You know our slogan: by helping others you help yourself most of all. The surprising thing is that that boy is already up to it. Only three days ago he was still drinking heavily. Of course he shows the marks of it. But at this stage he'll soon lose them. Everything's easy at his age."

Art burst into his characteristically loud, rich laugh.

"I wish I'd had the sense to do what he's done," he went on, "and not wait so long before knocking off the bottle! I hadn't even the excuse of not knowing Alcoholics Anonymous existed. More than twenty years ago, in their early days, a friend took me to see Bill W., their founder. He's a tremendous fellow. Have you met him?"

"Several times," I said. "He told me how it all began.

A. A. only had about a hundred members, and they met in Brooklyn, in a house lent to Bill by his wife's parents."

"Exactly," said Art. "Well, when I arrived on the scene, more ragged and stinking even than our friend here (Art waved toward the room where the tramp had gone), I had with me a flask full of the liquor you get in the Bowery—a poisonous brew if ever there was one. And while Bill and the others talked to me as if I were their brother and tried to rescue me, what did I do but pour the lot down my gullet. They had to put me outside. I wasn't an Irishman for nothing, and I was fighting mad. So I went back to the Bowery and its lousy slums. And to prison. And delirium tremens."

"What finally drove you to appeal to Alcoholics Anonymous?" I asked. "Poverty? Illness? A woman?"

"None of them," said Art. "My first wife had left me a long time before—and how right she was! Poverty? There's always some odd job you can do for a few hours in that place, or a sucker to borrow a small sum off— enough to buy the poison with. Health? I was made of iron."

"Well, what was it then?"

Art took his pipe out of his mouth and gazed thoughtfully for a moment at the glowing ash in the bowl. I noticed how remarkably handsome he looked.

"Then came the war," he said. "I had a deep love for this country and loathed everything Hitler stood for. I thought to myself: 'Now's the moment to prove that a drunkard can also be a man,' and I joined up. I was at a training camp for two months, and I drank nothing but water. I was in magnificent physical form; I was proud of being a soldier, I was happy. Then we were given weekend leave, and I went and got blind drunk. They discharged me from the army for disgraceful conduct. Yes, I was unworthy to defend my country. When I understood what had happened, I also understood—to use our A. A. slang—that I'd touched rock bottom. It was up to me to clamber up again."

Art had told me his story with typical simplicity, detachment, and gentleness. But I could guess from an indefinite tremor of voice and features how deep must have been the wound to the masculine pride of a man so strong and brave by nature.

Art shrugged his powerful shoulders, laughed, and said:

"So you see, it takes a world war at the very least to make some people sober!"

The telephone rang. The switchboard operator plugged in a line. Of the three electric bulbs fixed to the wall above her, it was the green one which went on—the one which corresponded to Art's table.

"My turn to play," said he, taking the receiver off his telephone.

He listened attentively, made the caller repeat his name and address, wrote them down carefully, and then said:

"O.K. Stick to it. Someone from here will be with you in an hour at the latest."

Art went up to the huge plan of New York on one of

the walls, and as he looked for the reference letters for the street he wanted, he said to me:

"This man has come out of the hospital after being disintoxicated for the sixth time. Up to now he thought he could manage alone. Now he realizes he can't, what with evening coming on and his desperate craving for drink increasing every minute, and he wants an A. A. member to support him."

When Art had located the little flag representing the group he needed, a group in Queens, a suburb a long way from where we then were in Manhattan, he went back to his table and consulted the thick directory. In it, under each day of the week, were the names of the members of each group who were voluntarily sacrificing their leisure time and staying within reach of a telephone in case of an S.O.S. from some alcoholic in trouble.

There was no reply to the first two calls Art made.

"They must have been sent for directly by some other clients in distress," said Art.

He consulted the fat book again and dialed another number. This time his man was at his post, and after giving the necessary information he hung up, filled his pipe, stretched out his long legs and sighed:

"He'll be in good hands; that's obvious from the tone of the reply."

The white and red lights went on almost simultaneously. The hunchbacked accountant and the old elevator man repeated Art's procedure.

"Night's coming on; the boozers are getting the wind up," said Art.

"How late will your people stay with them?" I asked.

"As long as they have to," said Art. "Till morning very often. Then they have to go to work."

Heavy blundering footsteps were heard on the steps leading down to the basement from the road. The door was thrown open roughly and a short stocky man, with a thick mop of gray hair and no tie, came into the room. He looked around him with narrowed bloodshot eyes, letting them rest on the hunchbacked accountant for a moment, then on Art, and greeting each with a muttered oath. He evidently didn't like the look of either of them. Then, with an air of fierce determination that tightened his jaws but could not stiffen his legs, he staggered over to the table where the old elevator man was sitting and fell into a chair.

The charming old man passed his hand slowly over his rosy cheeks. The shadow of some recollection seemed to float in his kindly, mischievous eyes.

"Hell of a binge, eh, and a hell of a hangover, too?" he asked gently. "What can I do for you?"

"The Towns Hospital," answered his visitor.

His voice was harsh, grating, obstructed by phlegm.

"I want to be taken to the Towns Hospital. Im-me-di-ate-ly."

"Not a bad idea," said the old elevator man. "But can you afford it?"

I had just asked myself the same question. The

Towns Hospital was a clinic for disintoxication that worked in close co-operation with Alcoholics Anonymous on a nonprofit basis. For this reason the cost of a cure was comparatively low. All the same, there was a fee. And it must surely be beyond the resources of this unshaved, unwashed alcoholic whose filthy clothes were covered with suspicious stains.

He raised his aching, fuddled head to a position as nearly erect as he could manage, and asked:

"Afford, did you say? Afford what?"

"To pay for your spell in the Towns Hospital," replied the old elevator man.

"I've enough money to pay for anything I want; get that!" shouted the drunk.

One of his hands moved mechanically toward his pocket; then he let it fall, muttering:

"Not on me at the moment, it seems. If I even had a quarter left, I should be off on the booze again. But you need only call up my house."

He gave his name, address, and telephone number. His address was in one of the most expensive districts of New York. I turned to Art, who was watching the scene, puffing at his pipe, and asked him:

"You have to be rich to live where he says he does, don't you?"

"You do," said Art. "This client of ours may well be a millionaire. We've had richer men than him arriving here in an even more deplorable state."

"But why?"

"After a terrible drinking bout lasting for days and

days, they feel frightened of themselves. They know they haven't the courage to give up alcohol without help."

The old elevator man put back the receiver.

"O.K.," he said to the drunk. "Everything's in order. I'll take you to the Towns Hospital as soon as I'm through here."

"But. . . ."

"There's no 'but' about it," said the charming old man, and there was suddenly a surprising note of firmness in his quiet voice. "Go into the waiting room and have some coffee."

He took his "client" by the arm, and the millionaire joined the tramp next door.

The green light winked over the switchboard operator's head. Art put the receiver to his ear. After a few moments, he said:

"I quite understand, doctor. Certainly, doctor. One of us will be there very soon, you can count on that."

While Art took down the information, I asked him:

"Was that an alcoholic doctor asking for help?"

"That happens more often than you might think," said Art; "but it's a different matter this time. The doctor wasn't asking help for himself but for his brother. He can do nothing more for him, medically or morally. A. A. is the only hope. His brother agrees."

Art went over to the large plan of New York. While he was looking at it, two men came in, and he gave them a friendly greeting. They were middle-aged, well fed, and carefully and expensively dressed. One of them took the hunchback's place; the other went to the switchboard.

"It's time the nurse went back to work," said Art, returning to his table, "and the accountant to his books. These two fellows are both successful Wall Street financiers. Members of A. A. Now that their day's work is finished, they'll take over here."

And Intergroup went on functioning according to the methods and routine it had followed every day for years past. Two very rich men had replaced two less prosperous volunteers. It made no difference. They were just two more alcoholics like the rest, and their free time belonged to all other alcoholics without exception: those without worldly goods and those possessed of considerable wealth—as exemplified by the two sick men who were now sitting in the smaller room with the dilapidated armchairs.

The financier who replaced the little hunchback was a broad-shouldered man with beautifully manicured hands and a carefully waxed mustache. He sat at the table in the middle of the room, nearest to the door. So that it was up to him to deal with a slim young mulatto who came down the staircase with feline silent tread, carrying a guitar case under his arm, his fine smooth skin seeming to be of the same material and color as his velvet suit.

The musician gazed around him like an animal in pain, advanced uncertainly but with graceful, dancing steps toward the first person he saw, and stopped.

The Wall Street man smoothed his waxed mustache with a varnished fingernail, and said:

◇◇◇

"Well, hello! What can I do for you?"

"I've come for a rest," said the dark-skinned musician.

He moistened his dry lips with the tip of his tongue and began again:

"I've drunk so much the last four days and nights that I can't keep my hand steady on my guitar. I can't stop on my own. I need someone to help me."

The Wall Street man went on smoothing his waxed mustache. He looked at the young Negro in silence, and his expression conveyed friendship, amusement, and severity all at the same time. Then he suddenly asked:

"Got anything on you?"

"I—no—really I haven't," said the guitarist. But he had hesitated a moment too long.

"Hand it over at once," ordered the financier.

His voice had all the authority of the head of a firm accustomed to immediate obedience. The hand that had been stroking his waxed mustache was held out imperiously toward the young Negro. As if hypnotized, the musician took a flat flask full of whisky out of his trouser pocket and put it on the table.

"Fine," said the Wall Street man. "Go into the other room. You'll find some coffee there."

The black musician glided past us.

"Hello, Herb!" said Art. "Made up your mind this time?"

"Don't know yet," said the guitarist.

"Ben, take good care of him!" cried the big Irishman to the "newcomer."

"Sure I will, Art, don't worry," replied Ben.

Art knocked the ash from his pipe and said to me:

"Herb is a regular here. After every binge, he comes to us—then he begins again. Some day he'll come for good."

In the wretched waiting room a hesitant chord was struck on a guitar, and a voice as soft as velvet began singing the blues.

I would have liked to stay indefinitely in that basement on 39th Street. Its remarkable routine fascinated me. But I had another appointment. Just as I was leaving, the green light went on again for Art.

"Yes, I see," he said into the receiver with his usual composure. "Just over an attack of d.t.'s? And you're afraid, with night coming on . . . yes, I understand. And the address? Good. That's my district. I'll come along myself."

Art hung up, and said to himself rather than to me:

"I've got two hours before I have to be at my office. Ought to be enough. If not, I can always call someone else in."

"Could I come with you?" I asked.

He looked at me and burst into a loud laugh.

"Reporter's fever, eh? Oh, I understand, all right! But it's no use."

"Why not?"

Art leaned far back, tilting his chair against the wall as if to give material expression to the difference between the two of us.

"Because," he told me, "an alcoholic can only bear to see and listen to another alcoholic, especially when he's

in a critical state. He won't trust anyone else. Yes, yes,
I know, you've had a lot to drink in your day, and made
a fool of yourself, and woken up with hangovers. But
you're not an alcoholic. And the client I'm going to see
would *know* that at once. We have a sixth sense about
that sort of thing, you see."

Art laughed again, and went on:

"You think our friend from the Bowery didn't guess
you were disgusted by him? Perhaps not consciously,
but he absorbed the fact through those same pores
which were sending out such a filthy smell. And he
could never be the same with you as with me. Yet, to
look at us, I seem as healthy as you, don't I? And I'm
even the less alcoholic of the two of us, measured by
ordinary standards. I've drunk nothing but water for the
last eighteen years. However, the fact remains that I've
been in the Bowery, and our pal who came from there
knows it without being told. He's aware of it from the
way I understand him or respond—by a sort of sixth
sense perhaps, I don't know."

Art shook his head. He was quite serious now.

"That poor guy who's just come out of the d.t.'s won't
be a pretty sight," he went on. "I don't suppose you've
any idea of what an alcoholic in the middle of a bout
can be like. The revolting, sordid room. The mixture of
sweat, cheap gin, fever, and vomit. Dirty clothes everywhere. Empty bottles lying all around, and full bottles
standing within reach. Well, even if the poor fellow is
half out of his mind, he'll recognize me as a brother, and
so he would one of these financiers dressed to the

teeth and smelling of expensive shaving lotion—but you, no—no go, I'm afraid."

My disappointed expression made Art burst out laughing. He slapped me on the back.

"To cheer you up, I'll make you a present of a good story, as we say in the trade. Here it is: a client at the end of his rope telephones here, urgently asking for help. We send him someone. Meanwhile, that boozer has emptied another bottle. When the A. A. member arrives at his house, he has no recollection of having sent for him. He picks up his shotgun and kills him outright.

"The murderer is put on trial. The victim's wife does all she can to save him. She knows he ought to go free; she says he's a sick man, that's all. When her husband was drinking like a madman, he might easily have done the same thing in the middle of a bout. Result: the murderer gets off with only a year. Today he's one of the best and most reliable of A. A. members."

Just as I was saying good-by, Art held me back.

"All the same," he said, "I can take you somewhere that ought to interest a journalist: to Bellevue. There's an A. A. group there, and I'm to speak to them next Friday."

The telephone bell rang. The financier at the switchboard plugged in a line. Green light.

"Hello!" said Art.

XII

Sing Sing

I stood at the edge of the pavement, studying the many-colored stream of close-packed automobiles. Three days earlier, Eve M., public relations officer of A. A., had said to me:

"You'll have to keep your eyes open next Sunday. The car won't be able to stop more than a moment, so you must be punctual. Exactly at noon a black 1958 Chevrolet will come along, driven by a thin gray-haired man. His name is Arthur G. He's already been informed, and he'll pick you up."

These instructions weren't as mysterious as they might appear. The only reason for them was that the traffic flowed in an uninterrupted stream past the corner of 58th Street and Fifth Avenue (where my hotel was), and no parking was allowed. All the same, there was one unusual feature about this rendezvous. The black Chevrolet and the gray-haired driver were going to take me to Sing Sing prison.

For it was there, behind thick walls, locked doors, and barred windows, that the A. A. meeting I was to attend would take place.

As I studied the passing cars, I remembered what a surprise my friend Bob of the *Herald Tribune* had given me one evening. He was describing the different A. A. groups he had come across on his countless journeys as a reporter all over the United States. There had been California fruit-pickers in an open shed; ranchers from New Mexico or Arizona who traveled hundreds of miles across the desert every week to meet in the school or church of some remote village; uranium miners around the borehole.

And, finally, criminals in prison.

"But how can they?" I had asked Bob. "Do the authorities allow these meetings?"

"They encourage them for all they're worth," my friend replied. "If you're interested, Eve can easily arrange for you to go to one. Sing Sing isn't far from New York."

That was why I was waiting for a black Chevrolet that Sunday.

Exactly at twelve the car appeared, and a good-looking gray-haired man leaned out the open window. His eye caught mine. He mentioned my name, and I got in beside him.

Now we were driving through the suburbs of New York, and I had time to get to know Arthur G., who had been a member of Alcoholics Anonymous for more than ten years. Before that time, according to his own account, this alert elderly man, now so well-mannered and sensitive, had been reduced by drink to a complete wreck physically, morally, and mentally. It seemed to him quite natural that he should share his Sunday with the inhabitants of Sing Sing.

I asked him if I should have any difficulty in getting in.

"None at all," said Arthur G. "As a rule, three people speak at each of our meetings, as you know; this afternoon there'll only be two: Tom B., a friend I'm picking up on the way, and myself. You'll come in as the third. Besides, the prison authorities can't do too much for us."

We had reached the outer suburbs, where open fields alternated with country homes and their gardens.

"Drink is one of the chief causes of crime in this country," Arthur G. went on. "A lot of people steal and commit assault or murder who would never have done such a thing if they hadn't been drunk or desperate because they couldn't satisfy their craving, or reduced to poverty by drink and unfit for any job whatever.

"The more intelligent and less hardened prisoners understand that. They have plenty of time for reflection in prison. Alcoholics of that sort realize that if they start drinking again as soon as they've completed their sentence, they will commit the same crimes and be shut up again. They also know that a prisoner who is let out on parole for good conduct isn't allowed to go into a bar. If he does, he will be imprisoned again immediately. They're anxious to give up drinking; but they haven't enough will power—they need help. That's what they get from Alcoholics Anonymous, first in prison and afterwards when they're free."

"How does it work out?" I asked.

"Just a moment," said Arthur G.

He had driven into a quiet side street edged with little white houses with velvety lawns. A short, rotund, muscular man of about forty was waiting in front of a fence. We stopped beside him, and he jumped in behind.

"Hello, Tom," said Arthur G.

"Hello, Art," said our new companion.

I was briefly introduced, and we went on our way. Then Arthur G. said:

"Tom, you're more up on the facts of A. A.'s work in prisons than I am. Our friend here would like a few details."

Tom B. leant forward from the back seat of the Chevrolet, and I felt the impact of his overflowing, magnetic vitality.

"Three figures will be enough," he said. "Today there are 355 prison groups of Alcoholics Anonymous. The oldest is in Ohio. They've just celebrated their thirteenth anniversary, and have 500 members. The most recent is Wyoming. As for our successes, listen to this: at San Quentin the proportion of alcoholics among the prisoners used to be eighty per cent before the formation of the A. A. group. Now it's dropped to forty-one per cent."

"So you see, it's quite natural that the prison directors

◇◇

welcome ex-drunks like us with open arms," said Arthur G., laughing.

"Even female members of Alcoholics Anonymous are admitted to Sing Sing," said Tom B. "Before that, no woman had ever penetrated its walls."

The sides of the hill were bare. At its foot flowed a wide gray river. On top of it was a compact mass of gloomy buildings. This was Sing Sing.

There have been so many films about prisons that it is not necessary for me to describe this one. It corresponded in every way to the pictures distributed all over the world: bars, cells, strong uniformed wardens —even a jovial, good-natured chaplain.

We had a friendly reception, but all the same we had to submit to a thorough search, and a pocket knife and a nail file had to be left behind in the office. Every gate and door we went past in our journey through interminable corridors was locked behind us. The sound of locking doors is the most depressing in the world.

We came out into a small inner courtyard. A burst of excited shouts was heard in the distance.

"On Sunday afternoons the prisoners play volleyball," said the warden.

"And there's television, the library, cards, or chess for those with different tastes," said the chaplain.

Tom B. turned his square energetic face toward me.

"Which shows," he said, "that the boys here don't just come to A. A. meetings out of boredom or because they have nothing else to do."

◇◇

"The boys come because they need to," said the Sing Sing chaplain quietly. "Here you are. See you later."

The door of a barrack with roughcast whitewashed walls opened and shut behind us.

There were between thirty and forty of them in a large room lighted by the sun streaming in through barred windows; the room was ordinarily used as a classroom to judge from the maps and blackboards on the walls. There were between thirty and forty of them in their prison dress, quietly sitting in two neatly arranged rows of chairs.

When we came in, they got up and remained standing until we reached the table at the end of the room. At one corner of this table was sitting a lanky mulatto of uncertain age, with a pair of thick glasses on his nose: the secretary of the Sing Sing group of A. A.

The other prisoners, Negroes and whites mixed, sat facing us; they were mostly young and presented an astonishing variety of facial expressions. This prison schoolroom seemed to provide samples of the entire range of the simplest, crudest, and most elemental human characteristics. Violence sat side by side with indolence, corruption with innocence, courage with cowardice, brutish stupidity with sly cunning, indifference with distress, resignation with defiance.

I particularly remember two young men: the flattened broad-nosed childish face of a Negro, and beside him a head set on a magnificent neck and covered in short Titian-red curls, the complexion and profile of a marble statue, and brilliant but cold, violet-blue eyes full of ruthless determination—the face of a fallen angel.

But as soon as the meeting began, all these completely different individuals were united by a single common impulse: with what concentration the members of the Sing Sing A. A. listened!

I had stopped counting the meetings of Alcoholics Anonymous I had attended; at every one of them I had been amazed by the seriousness and attentiveness of the audience. One or two of them had left particularly deep impressions on my mind.

There had been the A. A. group in Greenwich Village. I had been literally spellbound by the story of a young woman destroyed by drink, who had three times tried to commit suicide—with a revolver, by opening one of her veins, and by gas.

And a Harlem basement full of hypnotized men and women, where I was the only white man and where a man's rich, resonant, velvet voice confessed how he (the son of a clergyman) had been so ruined by drink and reduced to such despair that he had denounced God as a bastard and a son of a bitch.

But I could remember no audience whose concentration was so solid, so intense, so complete as that of the motionless forms dressed in prison garb gathered together that Sunday afternoon at Sing Sing.

It was because the terrible prison routine gave them time—long, heavy hours—to think of their problem as other alcoholics could not. And also because this routine was broken into by the arrival of men who had come from the world outside and who would return to it; decent, prosperous men who treated them as equals and comrades suffering from a disease. These were neither preachers nor philanthropists: they were simply alcoholics speaking to other alcoholics.

One after another, they said:

"My name is Arthur G. and I am an alcoholic."

"My name is Tom B. and I am an alcoholic."

The men who said this would in the course of a few hours be back in the great city, masters of their own movements, pleasures, and affections; yet they were talking to thieves, swindlers, forgers, and thugs, shut up within prison walls for years and years, as if they were equals and comrades.

These two men preached no sermons and drew no morals. There wasn't a hint of censure in what they said. They simply told the stories of their lives.

For in Sing Sing or on Park Avenue, whether the group was composed of millionaires like the "Minks and Sables" or of hardened criminals, Alcoholics Anonymous approached the subject in exactly the same way. But the prison setting gave a special resonance and significance to the stories told simply and without self-pity by Arthur G. (now a respectable tradesman) and Tom B. (an important official) of the terrible days when they were without money or job, ragged, half mad, denizens of the gutter, asylums, hospitals, and police stations.

And if they didn't say so in so many words, everything in their stories proved without a shadow of a doubt that they, too, had been potential criminals.

It would have taken very little, an intangible factor only, to have condemned them to the same fate as their audience. A blow need only have been struck a little harder or a wallet been more tempting; a policeman need only have been more spiteful, or a judge less understanding.

"So you see, we're not any different from you; we were just like you are. And you can become like us."

This was the truth underlying every change of fortune described by the two free men to the Sing Sing prisoners. And it was also why the prisoners listened to the stories with such unparalleled attention.

When the meeting was over, the prisoners surrounded Arthur G. and Tom B. and asked them questions. But the boy with the face of a fallen angel came up to me.

"Why haven't you spoken to us?" he asked, looking at me fixedly.

'I don't know enough English," I said with some embarrassment. "I come from Paris."

"Paris," the prisoner repeated after me.

There was a momentary sparkle in his cold blue eyes before they became inscrutable again.

XIII

At Random

I was dining with an American friend, a famous theatrical producer, and his wife in one of the best French restaurants off Fifth Avenue. If there was no one at the other tables, it was only because of the hour; for I had especially asked them to come early.

"Why all the hurry?" my friend asked. "Are you going to a show?"

"No—or rather, yes."

"Which means?"

"The performers at this show are ordinary people. It's an A. A. meeting in the Bowery."

Most people in the United States have heard of Alcoholics Anonymous and know its objectives and the nature of its activities. So that I was surprised by my friend's reaction.

"A. A. . . . ," said the producer.

He spoke so softly that I hardly heard him. One of

his hands rubbed at the short grayish mustache which emphasized the line of his handsome sensual lips. With the other he snatched hold of his double martini.

His wife said nothing. But there was so definite a look of appeal in her eyes that I obeyed a sort of telepathic impulse and asked:

"Why don't you come, too? The meeting is open to everyone."

The producer raised his handsome head, with its sensitive expression, as if to reply. But his wife forestalled him.

"What a good idea, don't you think so?" she said to him. "We've got nothing to do after dinner. And you're always looking for new situations and new characters. . . ."

She added, with a rather forced laugh:

"And luckily the dress I'm wearing tonight will do for any occasion. As for the rest. . . ."

She quickly divested herself of her valuable necklace and bracelets and put them away in her bag.

This Bowery meeting was like all others in that haunt of despair, with its depressing décor, its rank smell, the wasted ragged bodies and ravaged faces of the audience. But the presence of my friend made it different for me.

He was ordinarily a very highly strung man, incapable of keeping still for more than a few moments, yet I saw him sit the whole meeting through as if turned to stone on his metal chair. Elbows on knees and chin between his hands, he listened with almost hypnotized seriousness to the dreadful stories coming from the platform. It was as if every word left a mark on his flesh.

Then some remembered impressions of our early meetings came back to me: first in London during the war, then on a journey across defeated Germany just after the allied victory. He was drinking heavily—really heavily. I didn't pay much attention at the time. There were many others, including myself, doing the same. . . .

But I was disturbed by his attitude this evening. I knew that he had undergone treatment in a psychiatric clinic. "Overwork, nervous exhaustion," they had said. But was that all?

The words "allergy, chain reaction, obsessions" were echoing through the sordid hall, as at so many other A. A. meetings.

Was my friend one of those who must keep away from alcohol entirely or risk total catastrophe? But, in the A. A. vocabulary, he was in command of his own life. Better still: he was going from success to success. Yet I had been told of a hundred cases in which a man predisposed to alcoholism suddenly tottered and lost his balance at the very height of some brilliant achievement, and slithered down the slope that led to the Bowery.

When the meeting was over, the famous producer, walking like a man in a trance, went up to the A. A. member who had directed the proceedings. They talked apart for a long time. It is impossible to describe the anxiety and hope that appeared in turn, or sometimes

◇◇

both together, on his wife's face during this conversation.

This time the A. A. meeting was in Greenwich Village, the home of genuine and spurious artists and rich and poor bohemians; a region where moral licence is pushed as far as it can go.

Near me sat two youths with soft eyes and feminine mouths, filling in the time till the meeting by talking together in low voices.

"Before I joined the group, I'd got so that I couldn't read the newspaper," said one of them. "My hands used to tremble, and I couldn't distinguish the letters."

In the middle of the room was an elderly woman wearing men's clothes, with her white hair cropped short; she was chain-smoking, using the longest cigarette holder I ever saw. Her clean-cut profile showed exceptional intelligence and sensitivity.

"She's been coming to the meetings for the last twenty years," said my friend Bob. "Ever since they picked her up from a doorway more dead than alive."

The first speaker had taken the floor and everyone was listening in deep silence, when a huge man with unkempt red hair and shirt open to show his shaggy chest suddenly appeared framed in the doorway. He was drunk, but with a sort of bacchanalian dignity. He stared at the audience and growled contemptuously:

"You make me sick, you pack of fools! No one but Catholic Irish homosexuals could believe in such nonsense!"

After which he left.

◇◇

Bob chuckled.

"He's a painter," he said. "And an Irishman and a Catholic himself. He often bursts in on us like this. But it only proves that A. A. have him interested and already have had some effect on him. . . ."

"He never starts a row?" I asked.

"That guy? No, never," Bob said. "Some of the other drunks are a tougher proposition. Then they're turned out—by force, if necessary. In districts where such difficulties arise, A. A. always have a few reliable boys ready in case. Not the rough sort who clear people out of night clubs, of course. They never forget they were once drunks themselves."

Toward the end of my stay in New York an evening came when Bob rebelled against my ceaseless questions:

"Haven't you had enough of these appalling, sordid case histories that make up the very texture of our daily experience? Well, for my part I want to forget about them today."

He glanced at my face and began to laugh.

"Oh, all right," he said, "if I thwart your cannibalistic instincts too much, you may become dangerous! You shall have a story, but this time—I'm sorry—it's going to be a cheerful one."

Bob poured himself a cup of coffee (he drank it incessantly) and began:

"Last year a handsome and good young man called Andrew P. married a good and beautiful girl called Iris. They adored one another. But one day Andrew went out with some friends, drank more than he should have, and couldn't resist the charms of a waitress.

"Next morning, sober and disgusted with himself, Andrew arrived at the door of the little studio that contained all his happiness. What was he going to say to his loving and innocent young wife? How could he explain his absence all night? What feelings should he appeal to so as to be forgiven as quickly and as completely as possible? Andrew remembered the solicitous anxiety Iris had always shown for her darling husband's health. Yes—that was the chord he must touch. . . .

"Andrew opened the door and threw himself on Iris's mercy. He had never dared tell her before, for fear of losing her love—but now he must confess that he was an alcoholic. He had believed he could resist his vice, but suddenly the demon had got him again. . . .

"Andrew's calculations were not wrong. Iris stopped reproaching him for his absence. She had only one obsession now: Andrew must be saved from the abyss. She knew about A. A. and the results they had obtained. Andrew must join them. She would forgive him on that condition. Andrew accepted without hesitation. He had hardly hoped to get away with it so easily."

Another cup of strong black coffee, and Bob went on:

"So here was Andrew—who had never had the slightest problem with drink—joining Alcoholics Anonymous and becoming one of their most assiduous members. Iris saw to that: she went everywhere with her husband, to beginners' meetings and group meetings, for three whole months.

"Then came the moment when, according to custom, Andrew was told by his sponsor that it would soon be his turn to address a meeting, which meant, as you know, telling the story of his demoralization by alcohol. But though it had been easy for him to pretend up to that time, he felt quite incapable of producing a confession and making up a fictitious life story full of relapses and ignominy for the benefit of a large audience. So he said that he wasn't ready yet, that he was too nervous to appear on the platform. He was given a week's respite. And then another. After which his sponsor, the president of the group, and the friends he had made there all took turns bringing pressure on him.

"What could the poor guy do? He confessed. 'I'm dreadfully sorry,' he said, 'but I've never been an alcoholic. It was all because of Iris. Because I didn't want to hurt her. . . .'

"The other A. A. members showed great understanding and sympathy. They went against all the principles of the association and told Iris that her husband had no further need of them, since he was completely cured.

"So the marriage was saved."

The second annual congress of Alcoholics Anonymous for the southeast district of New York was held in a vast lecture hall in the Washington Irving High School. Hundreds of people, not all alcoholics, were present. The more important papers, such as the *Times* and the *Herald Tribune,* and the different radio networks had all sent reporters.

◇◇◇

The first speeches from the platform came from two famous specialists in mental illness.

One was a professor of psychiatry and medicine at Bellevue. He admitted that after twelve years of treating alcoholics by all the most modern methods known to psychiatry he had failed to obtain a single cure. His most highly qualified colleagues had had no better results. But when he came to follow the career of the patients he had failed to cure, after their discharge from the hospital, he was amazed to discover that *forty per cent* of them had become sober within four or five years solely as a result of joining Alcoholics Anonymous.

From that moment the professor began to apply the A. A. program to his own work. "But it's like a new language, and we scientists still have to learn it," he ended.

The second psychiatrist was director of a mental hospital in New York state. He had introduced a form of treatment derived from A. A.'s methods for alcoholics not suffering from specific psychological troubles. Result: out of 600 patients, 467 had been restored to normal life, and of these only 70 had had to return to the hospital.

The third speaker was an important New York judge. He declared that the general habit of putting alcoholics in prison in the United States was unjustifiable. It was the duty of society to consider alcoholism as a problem of public health, not a criminal matter. A. A. were doing excellent work to that end.

I made a note of these surprising figures and statements. My interest was constantly stimulated by some-

thing unexpected, picturesque, or pathetic in the
stories told by the Japanese, Irish, and Icelandic delegates; but they all suddenly seemed of secondary importance, insignificant almost, when a Negro member
of A. A., an officer in the American merchant marine,
began to tell us his latest adventure.

His freighter had put in at a large South African port.
The Negro didn't dwell on the regime of absolute, pitiless segregation that he had to submit to during their
stay. His listeners knew very well the universal fate of
colored men, women, and children in that country
where racialism takes the most bestial form it is possible to imagine. But no one in that hall could guess how
the story would end.

The first thing the Negro seaman did after landing
was to attend an A. A. group that had long existed in
the town.

He needed its help urgently. To be the object and
witness of this terrible discrimination was a powerful in-
ducement to get drunk. He had with him the big Alcoholics Anonymous yearbook, which contains the addresses of all groups and even isolated members
throughout the world, and he easily found his way to
the place he was looking for.

But there he was confronted by an astounding state
of affairs. Beside the Zulus, Hottentots, and Kaffirs,
whites were sitting. And this mingling enjoyed official
sanction. The apartheid government believed the work
of A. A. to be so important and fruitful that they made
in their favor a unique exception to the inexorable

◇◇◇

laws discriminating between South Africans according to the color of their skins.

Right at the bottom of Broadway, the avenue leading to ruin, at 267, a curious establishment is to be found among the flophouses and bars. It is called Sammy's Bowery Follies, and it has been there since the beginning of the century.

Inside is a spacious room with an enormously long bar on the left and a platform behind some rows of tables on the right. Tourists from all over Europe and America come here to have a look at the Bowery tramps, and the tramps come to get money for drink from the tourists.

I dropped in at the Follies alone one evening. All along the bar were sightseers and down and outs alternately: the former dressed in well-made clothes of good material, and wearing the rather smug expressions of people on holiday, with cameras slung over their shoulders; the latter with their rags, their dirt, their glazed eyes, and their morbid thirst. . . .

I was soon struck by the appalling monotony of the proceedings. The tourists tried to get the spectral figures to talk, and took photos of them; and the spectres endeavored to sell their remarks and to let the tourists photograph them in all their degradation for as many glasses of drink as possible. I went across to the other side of the room.

What was going on there was hardly more cheerful. An enormous old woman and a very thin old man were on the stage. Both were dressed in the fashion of 1900. A pianist, got up in the same style and so decrepit that he seemed about to crumble into dust, was accompanying their duet. Lugubrious parody—grim caricature.

Suddenly things seemed to liven up and take a frankly coarse and farcical turn. A popeyed policeman with crimson cheeks walked unsteadily past my table, lurched, knocked my glass over, staggered more wildly, caught hold of the nearest chair, miraculously recovered his balance, and glided off into the wings. Here was an actor with a real sense of the comic, even if he exaggerated the part a bit.

I said as much to the waiter who filled my glass of whisky. He stared at me, unable to speak for surprise.

"Actor?" he said at last. "What actor? That guy's a cop, a real cop, officially sworn in, on the level. And he's on night duty in the district. So of course we have to let him have plenty of booze."

"But then—then—" I said incredulously, "his billy?"

"All in order."

"And—there's a revolver in that holster?"

"Regulation, and fully loaded, you can take it from me," said the waiter.

As if in confirmation of his words, the policeman reappeared. His eyes were now vacant and staring, his face was a greenish color, and he was wiping his lips with the back of his hand. But he didn't make for the stage this time; instead he dragged himself to the bar and brought his fist down heavily on the metal top. He was given a large glass of neat Bourbon.

◇◇◇

Everyone, tramps and the rest, gave him a wide berth. Uneasy glances were instinctively going to the belt from which hung his billy and his revolver.

After swallowing his drink, the policeman went outside to get a little air in the avenue. He returned accompanied by another policeman, a Negro this time. They both leaned their elbows on the bar counter.

It was then that I remembered the A. A. group Bill W., the founder of the association, and Bob, my journalist friend, had told me about—a group composed entirely of policemen. I began to understand why this group was the only one among thousands which never admitted an outsider to its meetings, even if he were a member of Alcoholics Anonymous. For what revelations might not be expected from the complete confessions, in all their naked crudity, of men chosen for their physical strength, trained in the art of violence, drunk with power, always fully armed, who had once been desperate alcoholics?

The mere thought made my hair stand on end.

XIV

Of Wine and Roses

That Friday there was a meeting of Alcoholics Anonymous among the patients in Bellevue Hospital. Art, the big Irishman I had made friends with at Intergroup, had undertaken to get me in. We arranged to meet in front of the hospital.

I arrived early and I didn't regret it. The huge building overlooked the East River. The colossal bridges joining Manhattan and Brooklyn, the wake left by the ferries, the barges, pleasure boats, tugs, and swooping sea gulls all combined to make a fascinating spectacle, and the time of waiting passed quickly and happily.

Then I felt a heavy hand on my shoulder. Art stood before me, with his tall athletic figure, his youthful face (in spite of graying hair at the temples), and his pipe in the corner of his firm, smiling mouth.

"Have to wait a little," he said. "I'm expecting an ac-

complice, another A. A. member who's going to talk to
the folks."

Art turned his back on the river, with its ceaseless
activity, and contemplated the gloomy bulk of the hospital. Then he puffed once or twice at his pipe and began to laugh.

"I really must tell you about the first time I was shut
up here," he said. "I'd had my fill in the bars of this
district. I was blind drunk and in the middle of a bout.
The wife I was married to then, poor thing, found me
somewhere in the neighborhood, caught hold of me,
and tried to drag me home. No good. I shouted that I
wanted to kill myself, that I was going to jump into the
river. She believed me. We happened to pass a policeman, and she implored him to knock me out. He packed
a pretty good punch. A straight hit to the jaw, and the
next thing I knew I was up there among the crackpots
in a strait jacket.

"I ought to tell you that in this country an alcoholic
can't be shut up with madmen for alcoholism alone.
Even if the guy has gone right off the rails, or even if
he asks for it. The law insists that he must be a danger
to others or to himself. I had put myself in this last category. That's how I got there."

"Did you stay there long?" I asked.

"Long enough to be disintoxicated," said Art. "Physically disintoxicated, of course, that's all. The minute
they let me out I went across the road."

Art pointed to a vast building site on which the frame-
work of a skyscraper was being erected.

"A short while ago there used to be a terrible bar there, hidden between slum buildings, called The Bonfire. It was well situated. Guys like me, coming out after a cure, had only to cross the road. . . . Oh yes, The Bonfire. . . ."

Art broke off in order to wave wildly at an elderly gentleman, squarely built and very smartly dressed, who was just turning into our street.

"Bertie's an expert on madhouses," Art told me. "Before he came to A. A., he had been in Bellevue seventeen times, and fifteen times in various other asylums."

The old gentleman joined us. His face was burnt brick red by the sun, and he wore a short reddish mustache.

"I'm sorry," he said. "My train was late."

"Bertie lives in the country," said Art. "He owns several good horses and gives riding lessons to rich pupils."

We had reached the front doors of the hospital.

When we arrived at the sixth floor, where the patients were housed, the heavily padded door was opened cautiously and double-locked behind us. A long corridor led off to the left toward some rooms from which came strange cries and laughter.

"On the right," ordered the stout male nurse who had received us.

He showed us into a very small dining room furnished with a few chairs and a table, all made of metal.

I had never seen such a tiny A. A. meeting room. Nor such a small audience. Nor, above everything, such a disturbing one.

No, not even in Sing Sing.

There were six patients sitting on the other side of the narrow table, wearing hospital pyjamas and slippers. And it was impossible to distinguish among them those who were only temporarily deranged by drink and would soon leave Bellevue cured, and the organically, chronically insane, probably hopeless cases who would go on indefinitely trailing from asylum to asylum.

That old man, whose flabby jowls moved incessantly in a ceaseless silent monologue; those two living skeletons both tattooed with scabrous designs, one on his chest, the other at the base of his neck; that impassive bald Negro; that stout Puerto Rican and that muscular young man with the pleasant face—all of them showed signs of mental equilibrium mixed with the stigmata of insanity. One smiled too much, another's face was too expressionless. This one was a prey to nervous tics, that one to fits of trembling. But where and how could one draw the line between a temporary nervous disturbance and the total collapse of reason?

I wanted to ask my two companions for information, but it was some time since they had been to the hospital. They didn't know any of the patients and couldn't be sure of their exact condition themselves.

"We shall soon see from their questions after the meeting," said Art.

He was the first to tell the story of his career as an alcoholic. The six men listened to him in silence, with unflagging attention. There was nothing in their attitude to help one judge their state. It was the same when Bertie spoke in his turn. But at this moment I stopped asking myself which of the audience were mad and which were not.

A child had just come into the dining room: a marvelous little boy not more than ten years old, with a round intelligent face, creamy skin, shining black curls, and very lively eyes, full of courage and sweetness.

He was wearing slippers and pyjama trousers of the same material as the adults, but since the hospital was very warm he had taken off his jacket. His bare torso was golden brown as if it had been in the sun.

What was he doing here, this child from New York's Italian or Spanish quarter?

My first thought was that this little Sicilian goatherd or gypsy boy from Granada was here by mistake, that he had lost his way and belonged in another ward. But none of the patients seemed surprised to see him, and the little boy himself was perfectly at ease among them. He gave us a dazzling smile, came up to our table, took one of the cigarettes which Art had put there for the inmates, and lit it. He did this in the most natural and charming way, his eyes smiling with delight.

Quietly drawing in and puffing out the smoke in manly fashion, he followed Bertie's story with great attention and seriousness. Now and again he would shrug his small round naked shoulders, and his sensitive lips, curled around the cigarette, would whisper over and over again:

"That's it—yes—exactly like daddy. . . ."

As soon as Bertie had finished speaking, the hospital patients surrounded him and pressed him with questions. I now saw that the only madman present was the handsome young man I had taken for the sanest of them all. He believed himself to be a maharaja and an Arabian prince at the same time. All the rest were alcoholics, either beginning or ending a cure.

I had lost sight of the boy for a moment. Now I saw him oposite me. He took a cigarette from the table and then offered me one and lit it for me, as if apologetically. He did the same for Art.

"Tell me, sonny," the big Irishman asked him gently, "how the devil did you get into this place?"

The child gazed back at Art with soft shining eyes, fiddled with the knot that fastened his pyjama trousers around his little bare stomach, took a puff at his cigarette, and answered in an innocent, guileless tone:

"Because of my daddy. He drinks such a lot, and makes mummy and me so unhappy that I couldn't stay at home any longer. I had to find somewhere else to live, so I got a knife from the kitchen and I hurt one of my friends with it—oh, nothing much, and only in his arm. Then the police came for me and a doctor saw me and they sent me here."

"For a long time?"

Art was speaking in a tone I hadn't heard before from him, shortly and with detachment.

"I think," said the little boy playing with his pyjama cord, "I think I'm soon going to a state hospital in the country."

"Are you happy?" asked Art, still in the same uncharacteristic tone.

◇◇◇

"Not too bad," said the child. "The food's good" (he patted his smooth stomach); "it's quiet" (he lowered his voice); "the old man is a bit cross, but the others are nice. I'd much rather be here than at home."

We left. Art was silent. For the first time all the courage and cheerfulness had gone from his face. When we got to the place where The Bonfire used to be, he said gloomily:

"What a lot of harm an alcoholic can do to the people around him."

I remembered these words a week later.

It was in a setting quite unconnected with the hospital for the insane. I was at the top of a splendid, brand-new building on Fifth Avenue, sitting in a luxurious television room watching a play called *The Days of Wine and Roses.*

It had been produced with the co-operation of Alcoholics Anonymous, and showed how the habit and abuse of drinking changed, degraded, and ravaged the lives of a young man and a young woman who were good-looking, eager for life, and full of love for each other when they first got married. The simple human story, the realism of the detail, and the remarkably talented acting gave the screen tragedy a horrifying authenticity.

There were only two other people in the room with me: Eve M., whose official position had enabled her to arrange for the film to be shown, and her fifteen-year-old daughter Jane.

"She was very keen to see *The Days of Wine and Roses*," Even M. said to me before the film started.

When the last pictures had faded from the screen, I sat motionless for a few moments, still under their potent influence. Slowly the lights went on in the room. Then I saw beside me a fragile, delicate face that seemed to be hesitating between little-girlhood and adolescence, but with an expression of unusual and alarming maturity, the product of memory, suffering, and criticism.

"Yes—that's exactly it—that's exactly how I had to live," said Jane, separating each word from the last.

To whom was she talking? To me? her mother? or simply to her own terrible memories?

I couldn't help studying Eve M.'s face. That magnificently modeled tragic mask was expressionless. Only her huge eyes were blazing like diamonds darkened by pain. But they didn't avoid mine.

"Yes," said Eve M. clearly and distinctly, "that's the life my husband and I forced our children to lead. And it wasn't till I joined Alcoholics Anonymous that I fully realized what I was doing."

I turned toward Jane. Her fragile face seemed to have become thinner, and her pale cheeks were quivering.

As we left the television room, Eve M. said:

"I should like some strong hot coffee."

When we were sitting in a snack bar, she went on:

"Everyone knows or can easily imagine the torments the family of an alcoholic have to go through. But one

◇◇

curious fact has emerged from A. A.'s experience: the problem sometimes becomes harder to solve and the tragedy more acute when the alcoholic member of the family has stopped drinking."

I gazed at Eve M. in astonishment.

"I'm so sorry," I said, "but do you really mean what you've just said?"

"Every word of it," replied Eve M.

"But how can it be so?" I exclaimed. "How can the return to physical and mental health of a much loved man or woman make the family's troubles worse? Why should the fact that a lost soul has been saved intensify the drama? I don't understand. . . ."

"All the same, it's quite simple," said Eve M.

She smiled without gaiety and went on:

"Take the common case of the wife of an alcoholic who can't bring herself to desert him. What happens? She's the one who earns their daily bread; she's the one who makes all decisions and is responsible for business matters, house, and children. She becomes the man, the head of the family. If she manages all right, it's because the talent and the need to exert it were there potentially. Her husband's downfall and loss of will power give this talent the chance to blossom and be satisfied over a number of years.

"But then the man follows A. A.'s advice and program and gets back his strength, energy, and abilities. He can take his proper place in the home, and is eager to do so. All the more so because for fear of a relapse he has to fill up every moment of leisure or emptiness left by his disintoxication, and put to useful and healthy activity all the energy and passion he once used up in drinking and finding the wherewithal to drink.

"I expect you can guess the rest?" Eve M. said.

It certainly wasn't difficult. Now that he had recovered his sanity, his desire for activity, and the realization of his rights and duties, this man seemed an intruder, an usurper to the woman who had taken over his position of priority in the family during his defection. Hadn't she fed and cared for her fallen husband, and protected him against others as well as himself? And now suddenly he thought himself entitled to speak and act as her equal, or even her master!

"Things can reach such a pitch," said Eve M., "that women who have stoically gone on living with an alcoholic all through the time of his lowest degradation will leave him after he stops drinking. . . ."

"What happens when both husband and wife are alcoholics, and one of them gives up drink?" I wanted to know.

"There's bound to be a break," said Eve M., "The one who goes on drinking feels the other to be a traitor, a renegade. . . . And it doesn't only apply in marriage. I knew a very rich elderly woman with one adored daughter. They lived together and got drunk together. Then one day the daughter began to be afraid of alcohol and its effects. She took the decisive step of joining an A. A. group. Her mother threw her out of the house without a cent."

Eve M. finished her cup of strong black coffee, lit a cigarette, and gently shook her handsome head.

"You see," she went on, "the mechanism of these

situations is very simple. They arouse the most elemental feelings: protective instinct, desire for power or
complicity. Another emotion is often brought into
play: jealousy. Particularly in men.

"Imagine a husband who loves his wife and discovers
that she's an alcoholic. He tries everything to break her
of it—entreaties, demonstrations of affection, pre-
sents, appeals to all she holds dear. Nothing works. So
he accepts the situation. But he truly loves her, loves
her enough to go on cherishing her as she is—smelling
of wine, grown ugly, demoralized, shaken by d.t.'s—
and he surrounds her with attentions, sympathy, and
understanding.

"All at once or by gradual stages—it doesn't matter
which—he sees her begin to fight against her addiction, reduce its hold, and then conquer it entirely. He
ought to be the happiest of men. And so he would be if
her cure had been his doing, the result of his influence
and the love he gives her and inspires in her. But it's
nothing to do with him. Perfect strangers, members of
Alcoholics Anonymous, have had this effect on his wife.
She has made for others the sacrifice that she so obstinately and fiercely refused to make for him in spite of
all his tender care and entreaties. Then he begins to feel
jealous, and the poison spreads.

"According to temperament, it will take the form of
anger or cunning, be intermittent or chronic, normal or
abnormal. Sometimes it is even murderous.

"We all know the case of the rich handsome young
man who waited for his young wife to come out of an
A. A. meeting and shot her with his revolver."

◇◇

I was silent, trying to get used to this new aspect of
alcoholism in which disintoxication, not intoxication,
had become the crucial factor. Then I asked:
"Are you doing anything about this problem?"
"No," replied Eve M. "A. A. are not doing anything.
But there is an association inspired by ours and in close
touch with us which concerns itself with family matters. If you're interested, I'll make an appointment for
you with Lois, their secretary."

In an almost monastically bare office I found a little
elderly lady who radiated charm. She was delicate and
worn, but one felt that she possessed inexhaustible
and fathomless reserves of generosity, kindness, and
tolerance. She told me, with infinite good will, what I
wanted to know.

Her association was made up of the relations of
alcoholics—fathers, mothers, husbands, wives, brothers, or sisters. They weren't alcoholics themselves.
That did not mean they were abstainers. There was no
reason for them not to allow themselves wine, beer,
cocktails, and alcohol, for drink was not a vital and
dangerous problem to them.

They met together to study the best means of helping
someone they loved who was being destroyed by drink,
and at the same time to make family life easier.

The little old lady went to fetch a book explaining the
history and principles of the association. She wrote in
it and presented it to me, saying quietly:
"Everything I know I learned from Bill."

I wasn't sure what she meant by this, and I didn't

press the point. It was only when I was outside and opened the book and saw the frail old lady's signature on the flyleaf that I understood. I already knew that her Christian name was Lois. But after it I now found her surname, which began with a W and was the same as Bill's.

As that of Bill W., founder of Alcoholics Anonymous, with whom I had had so many long conversations; as that of Bill W., successful speculator on Wall Street, afterwards a chronic alcoholic, ruined, dying, half mad, and for many years supported, cared for, and protected by his wife Lois, who had a humble job as a saleswoman in a Brooklyn store.

When the gentle old lady said: "I learned everything from Bill," she meant that her love for him had taught her to endure the greatest pain and anxiety it's possible to suffer, in seeing the person she loved best in the world go downhill, lose his reason, and gradually commit suicide. And to understand, sympathize, and help him all the time. And also, when he had escaped from the abyss, to recognize that he came first and that she must now take her place in his shadow.

I turned the pages of the little book Lois W. had given me—and written herself, no doubt. The association for the families of alcoholics was ten years old. It had more than a thousand groups in the United States.

I shut the book again. The street was filled with the savage roar of that busy quarter of New York. Other figures passed through my mind. I thought of the 325

A. A. groups in mental clinics, visited every week by men whose only purpose and passion was to help their unfortunate brother alcoholics; I thought of the 255 prison groups, visited every Sunday by other men of equal ardor and faith—or by the same.

Faces came to my mind which didn't belong to any of the passers-by in this crowded street. Those of the Intergroup volunteers, who sacrificed their weekly holiday to receive the desperate appeals of alcoholics all over the vast city and send them help. And those of the women and men of every class and degree of wealth and education who were available at any moment of night or day to help poor wretches fight against the disease they had once suffered from themselves.

I thought of the still young, still beautiful woman covered with magnificent jewels whom I had met at a gala dinner, mainly for A. A. members. She told me that though she had been born into one of the richest American families, drink had reduced her to sleeping like a tramp on doorsteps and to shoplifting to pay for a few glasses of adulterated gin. Alcoholics Anonymous had restored her to life, and now she owned a famous dressmaking establishment. But she still worked indefatigably for the association.

She told me that the first group meeting she held took place in a particularly destitute and sordid area. The room was disgustingly dirty. The monotonous tunes of the jukeboxes in neighboring bars often drowned her voice. The audience consisted entirely of sodden drunks who had only come there so as to get

out of the snowstorm raging outside or to get a cup of
coffee or have a cigarette. She had had as assistant a
frail old man, who spent his time picking up anyone
who fell on the floor and sitting him on his chair again.

I remembered a story I had heard from a distinguished fighter pilot. He, too, had been brought to the
lowest possible stage of ruin by drink. He, too, had
been saved by A. A. But one day, his birthday, when he
was on board a freighter off the coast of South Africa,
he was suddenly overtaken by an appalling attack of
anxiety and distress. He was tortured by the longing
to resort to his old remedy—whisky, the philter that
brought unconsciousness. He felt that the next stop
they made, at Durban, would be fatal to him. So he
feverishly turned the pages of the Alcoholics Anonymous yearbook, and found in it the name and address
of the *only* member living in Durban, to whom he
cabled an S.O.S. And when he disembarked, a stranger
was waiting for him, and took him home and treated
him with brotherly solicitude until the crisis had passed.

"If it hadn't been for him, I should have been lost,
wiped out," said the ex-pilot.

The evening before I left, I had a last conversation
with Bob, the *Herald Tribune* journalist who had become my friend.

"How do you account for the fact that so many A. A.
members are full of life and energy, seem younger than
their years, and are so successful in whatever they
undertake?" I asked him.

"It's because they have had to have exceptionally good health to survive the massive doses of poison they have absorbed," said Bob. "And once they are free from this poison, their organisms gain new strength and youth. It's the same with their minds. They get back their old flexibility, acuteness, and need for activity. All the energy they wasted in getting hold of liquor, drinking it, and sleeping it off is suddenly available again.

And the instinct of self-preservation impels them to use these faculties to the full, so as never to leave any period of time unoccupied, any break in their defenses through which the old obsession could creep into their minds and bodies. That's the reason for the success you find so surprising.

"It's also the reason for what you call devotion, sacrifice, generosity, fellow-feeling, but which is really only a precaution against the ever-present threat of one's own failing."

"Whatever the reason, Bob," I said, "the facts are—remarkable. I have never before come across so much human warmth and understanding as I've found among Alcoholics Anonymous. It's as if their having known the uttermost depths of ruin and the darkness of night had made them superior to other men."

"Perhaps so," said Bob.

He spoke as simply and modestly as usual.

"Perhaps," he repeated. "But only on condition that the memory of their sufferings and degradation is kept alive and bleeding, and put at the disposal of everyone. In that case perhaps, an alcoholic has a better chance than other men of becoming the salt of the earth."

All that I learned from my investigations and have faithfully set down here has led me to believe that this is true.

APPENDIX

❧

Are You an Alcoholic?

Put the following questions to yourself, and answer them as honestly as possible.

1) Does your drinking keep you away from your work?
2) Does your drinking make your family unhappy?
3) Do you drink because you feel ill at ease with people?
4) Do you drink enough to affect your reputation?
5) Have you ever felt remorse after getting drunk?
6) Have you been in financial difficulties as a result of drink?
7) When you drink, do you get into bad company and frequent low haunts?
8) Do you neglect your family's well-being when you are drinking?
9) Have you lacked ambition since you took to drinking?
10) Are you obsessed with a longing to drink at certain times of the day?
11) Do you want a drink the morning after?
12) Do you find it difficult to sleep when you drink?
13) Have your abilities diminished since you began to drink?
14) Does drinking compromise your position or your business?
15) Do you drink to escape from worries or difficulties?

◇◇

16) Do you drink when you are alone?
17) Have you ever suffered from loss of memory when drinking?
18) Has your doctor ever treated you for alcoholism?
19) Do you drink in order to give yourself self-confidence?
20) Have you ever been in a hospital or institution because of alcoholism?

If you have answered "yes" to one of these questions, you are perhaps an alcoholic.

If you have answered "yes" to two of these questions, the chances are that you are an alcoholic.

If you have answered "yes" to three or more of these questions, you are definitely an alcoholic.

(This questionnaire is used at Johns Hopkins Hospital in Baltimore to determine whether or not a patient is an alcoholic.)

A NOTE ON THE TYPE

The text of this book was set on the Linotype in a new face called PRIMER, designed by RUDOLPH RUZICKA, earlier responsible for the design of Fairfield and Fairfield Medium, Linotype faces whose virtues have for some time now been accorded wide recognition.

The complete range of sizes of Primer was first made available in 1954, although the pilot size of 12 point was ready as early as 1951. The design of the face makes general reference to Linotype Century (long a serviceable type, totally lacking in manner or frills of any kind) but brilliantly corrects the characterless quality of that face.

A NOTE ABOUT THE AUTHOR

Joseph Kessel was born in 1898 on the Argentino pampa in a Jewish colony where his father was a doctor. He then lived in Russia, on the Ural River, until the age of ten, when he settled in France.

By the time he was eighteen and had volunteered for the French Air Force, Kessel had already studied at the Sorbonne and had worked as a reporter and as an actor. In 1918 the squadron he joined in Siberia took him for the first time around the world.

Between the two world wars, Kessel made a name for himself as a novelist, a widely traveled journalist, and a screenwriter. During the Occupation he worked for the Resistance until he was forced to escape to England, where he continued to rally for the Free French.

The Lion, published in 1959 by Alfred A. Knopf, was unanimously hailed as M. Kessel's finest novel.

January 1962